Praise for *The Power of Collaboration:*

"Thea Singer Spitzer has spent years getting under the bonnet of some of the world's most successful companies. Across the tech sector we see how collaboration can bring together ambitious individuals to become more than the sum of their parts. Spitzer's 'Silicon Valley Approach to Collaboration' shows how this dynamism accommodates individuals while uniting them in a shared purpose. *The Power of Collaboration* will be useful to anyone who wants to implement these strategies as it comes packed with useful examples and exercises to make it happen."

—Russ Shaw, founder of Tech London Advocates and Global Tech Advocates

"A helpful set of tools to deliver quality collaboration in any organization. The viewpoints and experiences of other companies was especially impactful!"

—Amy Hanlon-Rodemich, EVP, People Success, Milestone Technologies

"*The Power of Collaboration* is a how-to manual of Dr. Spitzer's transformational methods for improving collaboration across organizations small and large alike. Her book is filled with insightful gems that will make those applying them reach greater levels of teamwork."

—Darrell Blegen, Chief Product Officer, Finagraph

THE **POWER** OF
COLLABORATION

Powerful Insights from Silicon Valley to Successfully Grow Groups, Strengthen Alliances, and Boost Team Potential

THEA SINGER SPITZER, PhD

CAREER
PRESS

The Career Press, Inc.
Wayne, N.J.

THE POWER OF COLLABORATION
COVER DESIGN BY JEFF PIASKY
Printed in the U.S.A.

To order this title, please call toll-free 1-800-CAREER-1 (NJ and Canada: 201-848-0310) to order using VISA or MasterCard, or for further information on books from Career Press.

CAREER
PRESS

The Career Press, Inc.
12 Parish Drive
Wayne, NJ 07470
www.careerpress.com

Library of Congress Cataloging-in-Publication Data

CIP Data Available Upon Request.

DEDICATION

We awaken amazing power when we come together to create something even better than we could on our own.

ACKNOWLEDGMENTS

Although I am the sole author of this book, it is the product of much collaboration.

I owe a huge thanks to each of the 28 generous Silicon Valley leaders who willingly shared their time and thoughts, displaying just the sort of collaboration that was the topic of our conversation. This book would not be nearly as robust without their imprint.

Special thanks are owed to two people who demonstrated the meaning of collaboration in their willingness to go "above and beyond" to help me make connections with some of the leaders with whom I spoke. Those people are Mike Glass from Microsoft and Anne Hausler from Merit Resource Group. Each of them dug deep into their networks to connect me with leaders who personify collaboration. I am indebted.

Several other colleagues and friends deserve special mention. Ruth Nathan, a renowned author, assisted me in evolving general philosophies into practical concepts as we exercised our minds along with our bodies. Gail Finger was a professional sounding-board, someone with whom I could pilot-test ideas and my articulation of them. John Midgely added immeasurably with his perspective as an avant-garde leader. Eileen Zornow was invaluable in taking my ideas and turning them into graphics that did a great job of telling my story. Chuck Freedenberg has been an advisor to me for years. His thoughts on early drafts of this book helped crystalize my thinking.

Thanks to Marilyn Allen, my agent, who astonished me with the speed at which she found a willing publisher for my thoughts. Thanks, also, to the team at Career Press for believing in the importance of this story and helping get it out to the world.

Rosalind Warren is an accomplished author and editor extraordinaire. To call her my editor, though, would markedly understate the role she played in bringing this book to its current state.

Roz undertook this journey in a professional capacity. That wasn't the case with my husband, Craig Spitzer. He knew (better than I) what I was getting myself into in signing this book contract. What he may not have known was the degree that it would affect his life as well. He went along this journey with amazing grace, even though it was my dream and not his. Not only did he go along, he was actively involved every step of the way, often leading. Craig used his immense store of creativity to help me transform concepts into polished models. He used his sophisticated wordsmithing abilities to smooth and clarify my writing. And he did so much more.

To those others whom I am not calling out by name, I also owe a debt of gratitude. I hope you will understand and forgive not being named, and know how much I value and appreciate each of you.

CONTENTS

INTRODUCTION

HARMONIZING EMPLOYEE EFFORTS

Imagine eight musicians who are members of a renowned jazz ensemble diligently working on a new musical piece. If you could listen in on each of them individually, you would hear highly competent musicians, each practicing his or her part and sounding quite good.

Then they get together and, suddenly, something captivating happens: You hear and feel the piece come alive. It's no longer just several skilled performers. Their instruments blend into one rich, unified voice. The musicians are in unique dialogue with each other. It's "musicality."

Imagine those artisans making up a workplace team. Imagine that amazing collaboration coming together as an iPad. . . or TurboTax . . . or a winning basketball team. Our job—as employees and as managers—is to combine our individual and team efforts to make "music" like that.

Graphic by Eileen Zornow

If they do a terrific job, that music group might transport their audience . . . or win a Grammy. Similarly, that workplace team might make a lot of consumers, employees, and shareholders happy. If not done well, collaboration is a blueprint for a mediocre product or even a failed one. This failure is all too common in organizations. Individuals and teams may be extremely competent in their area of focus, but if they don't collaborate well with others, the final product will suffer.

During the last several decades, much progress has been made to foster better workplace collaboration. Nevertheless, getting people to work well together remains one of the tough issues that keeps both managers and individual employees up at night. We need to do better. If we continue to use existing tools, we only make incremental strides in addressing this snarly problem. We need a new model.

A NEW APPROACH TO COLLABORATION

Throughout the course of my nearly 30-year management consulting career, I've developed a number of specialties. Some came about because organizations needed help in those areas. Others were passions of mine. My expertise in collaboration is a confluence of both company need and my own passion. I've helped employees in many companies, across numerous industries, achieve more by working better together. I have received awards for collaboration programs I helped create at both Microsoft and telecom giant GTE (now known as Verizon).

After working with organizations in the greater San Francisco Bay area for a number of years, I began to notice that there is something different about the way their employees work together compared to other companies. There is something magical happening in Silicon Valley. Based on my observation and experience, I crafted the Silicon Valley Approach to Collaboration (SVAC). Then, I had conversations with 28 Silicon Valley leaders to fine-tune the Approach. The purpose of this book is to make that framework available to companies anywhere, to help employees come together and succeed brilliantly.

WHAT'S SO SPECIAL ABOUT SILICON VALLEY

The nickname "Silicon Valley" originated in the early 1970s to describe a district in the south San Francisco Bay area where a number of silicon chip manufacturers were concentrated. Over time it has grown. It now covers a much bigger geographic area ranging from the city of San Francisco in the north, to the greater San Jose metropolitan region in the south, and large swaths of the East Bay.

Along with its physical boundaries, its symbolic ones have also grown. Now, it is not only a catch-phrase referring to technology, bio-tech, and other assorted industries, it is also a metaphor for a particular work and life style.

Silicon Valley is renowned for building complex, successful businesses.

 ❍ It is still one of the leading creators of innovation. It
   produces more patents per capita than any other region
   in the world.[1]

- It continues to receive more investment capital than any other metropolitan region.[2]
- It has the third highest GDP of the top 300 metropolitan areas globally.[3]
- It is a big part of the reason why California's economy qualifies as the sixth largest in the world.[4]

Silicon Valley has earned its reputation by building cutting-edge innovations that help enrich people's lives; not just in the area of technology, but in many arenas that touch millions. It encompasses areas such as solar energy, high-quality health care, pharmaceuticals, and more.

Many people want to learn the secret of Silicon Valley's success. Part of that secret is the unique way that their employees work together. Companies in Silicon Valley have been successful because they did more than simply apply existing business models and tools. Without consciously realizing it, they began to create a new model for collaboration. I will explain that new model and show how any company can adapt it to help achieve its goals.

What makes Silicon Valley's approach to collaboration distinctive? Many employees there have a pragmatic view of people working together. They value results. They've seen these results happen when employees share ideas. They happen when employees adopt others' knowledge. They happen when employees honestly and respectfully engage in robust conversations that result in better decisions.

People working in Silicon Valley firms are aware of the potential downsides of collaboration. They know that work can sometimes take longer when more people are involved, especially when they have differences in views. They are aware that staff can temporarily lose focus on their own work when they pause to assist others. But, in weighing the benefits against the costs, they realize that when it's done right, the upsides far outweigh the downsides.

Thankfully, collaboration successes are not limited to companies in Silicon Valley. Lessons from this region can be applied to any firm, anywhere, to make it more successful. This book will set out the SVAC along with numerous examples illustrating how it looks when collaboration is done well.

WHY NOW

A new model for collaboration is particularly relevant right now. The number of people in the United States who feel drawn to those with similar beliefs and cut off from those who differ is growing. Rifts among people holding opposing views are creeping into the workplace. This is creating schisms and reducing trust between staff who used to work well with each other. In some instances, it is increasing an "us versus them" way of thinking, alienating folks from others, and making collaboration more challenging.

People want to fix this. Some think that to improve collaboration the rifts need to be resolved first. Fortunately, that is not the case. Successful collaboration calls for an open dialogue of deeply held views in a way that maintains trust and fuses divergent perspectives into great solutions. The philosophies and practices embedded in the collaboration approach offered in this book will help lessen those schisms and reduce "us / them" thinking while building a collaborative culture.

WHAT YOU WILL FIND IN THIS BOOK

Chapter 1 sets the stage with a definition of collaboration. It explores the importance of collaboration to any company. Chapter 2 reveals several important characteristics and beliefs shared by people who are committed to collaboration. Some of them might surprise you.

Your journey into the world of Silicon Valley collaboration intensifies with Chapter 3, which will immerse you in several examples of highly successful collaborations that the leaders interviewed for this book shared with me.

Chapter 4 rolls out the SVAC. This chapter provides an overview of the Approach and its three levels of focus: individual skills, team tools, and company practices.

The rest of the book offers an in-depth look at the individual skills, team tools, and company practices that will bring this model to life at your company. Chapters 5, 6, and 7 explore the individual skills. Chapters 8 and 9 roll-out the team tools. Chapters 10, 11, and 12 focus on company practices. Chapter 13 shares the secret sauce of the company-wide Collaborative Ethos that will result from using this approach. Chapter 14 wraps up with a suggested process to guide your next steps.

THE SILICON VALLEY LEADERS WHO CONTRIBUTED

In writing this book I interviewed 28 Silicon Valley leaders who were generous enough to share their experiences with me. The book would be less vibrant without their input. Of course, you will want to know who those leaders are. You can find them in the following chart.

Although participants are shown with the firm with which they were associated at the time of the interview, most of their responses incorporated broader experiences collected throughout the course of their careers with a number of Silicon Valley companies. The examples they shared with me reflect their own point of view rather than any official company perspective. A few of the narratives have been attributed to them and their company (with kind permission). The rest are shared anonymously to preserve the privacy of the firms and the people employed by them.

These 22 leaders, and six others who chose to remain anonymous, represent a wealth of knowledge about the ways Silicon Valley companies leverage employee collaboration. These leaders are in a variety of professions, and their ages span several decades. Their current employers range in size from several hundred employees to more than 100,000. Some of these firms are self-contained in the Silicon Valley area. Others have multiple presences nationally or globally. Diverse industries are represented, including social media, entertainment, health care, pharmaceuticals, automotive, finance, electronics, gaming, toys, technology, retail, commerce, and many others.

Leader Interviewed	Employer
Leaders Employed at One Company	
Gisela Bushey	SanDisk
Adam Clark	Electronic Arts
John Donaldson	Pandora
Marianne Franck	Cisco Systems
Jorge Glascock	Genentech
Mike Glass	Microsoft (for his deep leadership expertise in Agile)
Amy Hanlon-Rodemich	Milestone Technologies
Doug Haslam	Lucid Motors
Jake Huffman	Intuit
Gillian Kuehner	The Permanente Medical Group (Kaiser Permanente)
Jim Marggraff	Google
Michael Mulligan	Mechanics Bank
Lawrence Nathan	Kaiser Permanente
Jason Scovil	Facebook
Paul Valentino	Rambus
Leaders Working With Multiple Companies	
Munir Bhimani	MBLOGIC LLC
Ron Lichty	Ron Lichty Consulting
Clint Lynch	Silicon Valley Executive
Madeline Schroeder	StudyAce
Russ Shaw	Founder, Global Tech Advocates & Tech London Advocates
Doug Walton	DNA Global Network
Kimberly Wiefling	Co-Founder, Silicon Valley Alliances, and Author

By the end of this book you will have learned a cohesive approach to collaboration that is practical and adaptable to any company's needs. What I won't burden you with are extended exposés of systems and behaviors that kill collaboration. Most of us know the pain of such situations and don't need a book that stresses what not to do. This is about what can be done.

Let the journey begin.

1

THE POWER OF COLLABORATION

Many of the amazing things that have defined us were created by people in collaboration with others. The United States Constitution was crafted by 39 men working together. Marie and Pierre Curie won a Nobel Prize for their discoveries regarding radiation. James Watson and Francis Crick worked with Maurice Wilkins and Rosalind Franklin to decode the secrets of DNA. On another note, John Lennon, Paul McCartney, George Harrison, and Ringo Starr came together and changed popular music forever.

Collaboration in business is just as important. For instance, it made an enormous difference in the launching and running of LinkedIn. Reid Hoffman could have started the company on his own, but knew it would be more likely to be a game-changer if he teamed up with several colleagues. He did, and today, LinkedIn boasts more than 500 million members globally. Collaboration is still a defining feature of how their employees perform their work.[1]

Imagine our world without these and many other discoveries that came about because people were able to blend their individual expertise into collective intelligence to accomplish amazing things.

It is in our nature as human beings to collaborate. Evidence from the earliest agricultural era, 10,000 years ago, confirms that people lived in communities and combined their efforts. Even back then, people were better off pooling their talent and resources with others, rather than going it alone.

Although people have known about and used collaboration for a long time, our search for ways to make it more effective in workplaces is fairly recent. Since the latter half of the 20th century, corporate leaders have been trying to bring employees together more effectively. This doesn't mean doing everything as a team or discussing things ad nauseam until complete consensus is reached. It simply means coming together when it adds value and produces better outcomes than we can achieve on our own.

THE BUSINESS IMPERATIVE

The question is not "Is your company doing well?" Rather, it is "Could you be doing even better?" There are very few companies that can honestly answer that question in the negative. However successful a company is, most could be even more successful.

The demand for innovations that delight customers is constant. What does that have to do with collaboration? As marketing expert John Ward put it, "Innovation and collaboration go together like . . . well, like Batman and Robin. Just like that dynamic duo . . . innovation and collaboration are more powerful together."[2]

Imagine a group of renowned chefs coming together to create an extraordinary multi-course banquet for a special event. What if each of them is asked to prepare their signature recipe for the course assigned to them. The trouble is that there is no time for those chefs to talk with each other and design a menu in which all the dishes complement each other. When the appetizer, soup, salad, entrée, vegetable, and dessert are served, there is little chance that this meal is going to be a palate-pleasing experience.

This example might seem too far-fetched to actually happen in a workplace. Yet it's all too accurate a description of things that have occurred over the decades, and still do happen. Picture how different that dinner could have been if those chefs had the chance to chat and decide on courses that not only tasted wonderful on their own, but also fit well together. As some of them realized that their recipe didn't fit the theme they would have prepared something else for the good of the dinner.

Study after study reports that staff believe their company would benefit if employees worked together better. In a 2005 McKinsey Quarterly study, 80 percent of senior executives said they knew that successful collaboration across product, functional, and geographic lines was crucial. Yet, only 25 percent of them rated their own company effective in this regard.[3]

Much has been learned about fostering collaboration since that study. Yet we still have plenty of room for improvement. In a 2015 survey, senior leaders at a variety of companies still cited poor collaboration between employees as one of the biggest threats to their company's success.[4]

The good news is that most people now recognize the need for collaboration. Businesses see that the failure to collaborate hurts them, and they've acted on it. Most leaders are trying to bring employees together when it makes sense. They are doing much better at this than they did in the past. For instance, engineers, sales and marketing professionals, and finance and other experts increasingly come together to design, manufacture, and sell products that thrill customers.

The challenge is that just bringing staff together doesn't guarantee that they will automatically be able to leverage their collective intelligence. There is opportunity to help those people be even more effective when they come together. When it works well, something astonishing happens. Individuals actually start to "interact as components of a larger mind . . . you [create] a communal brain."[5] That creation of communal brain is at the heart of truly effective collaboration.

DEFINING COLLABORATION

How do you define collaboration? Give some thought to this question before you read on.

Now let's look at how some Silicon Valley leaders defined it when they spoke with me:

- "It's how we work together when we're not directed to; when we are contributing as a group of people."
- "Leaders and employees all engaged together, sharing information, ideas, goals, pretty much everything. . . . Transparency is really important—allowing people to see the bigger picture and the details. When there's a problem or challenge, working together to solve it, instead of playing the blame game."
- "Cooperating; not only within our functional group. Working up, down, within, and outside. . . . Being holistic in our view and in how we communicate it. Figuring out how to knock down walls that are getting in the way. How to foster great ideas rather than kill them."
- "Asking myself: 'How can I help you?' versus 'What am I going to get out of this for myself?'. . . . 'How can I help build trust quicker?'"
- "Sharing in a way that moves the team forward effectively, creatively, with better results."

One secret of Silicon Valley's success starts with a nuanced understanding of what it means to work together. Employees across the organization see the value of collaborating and combining their knowledge.

Accordingly, the definition for *collaboration* throughout this book is: "Being willing and able to blend our ideas and efforts into a 'communal brain' to create better results by working together than we could on our own."

There are times when working with others will yield much better results. At other times working on our own is the better option. When working with others is optimal, we need to harness the strengths of everyone involved in ways that will help us achieve our shared goals.

INTERACTIVE NATURE OF THIS BOOK

The purpose of this book is not just to communicate concepts but also to facilitate your use of them. To help you achieve that goal, at various points throughout the chapters, I will suggest activities to assist you in applying the concepts. When you see the word *application* in a shaded box, you will know that you're at one of those points. I encourage you to create a dedicated workbook or journal to record your responses.

When you get to Chapter 14, I will help you translate your thoughts into a description of the current state of collaboration at your company. I will also share initial steps you can take to help "move the needle" and assist your firm in fostering even better collaboration. Constructive change is often initiated by employees who have a vision for how things could be better and a passion for helping to bring about that change. By observing and insightfully piecing together what might be, you can help your company leverage employee intelligence even more successfully.

 APPLICATION

Now that I have shared Silicon Valley's definition of collaboration and the definition that will be used throughout this book, it's time for your first activity. Ask five colleagues how collaboration is currently defined at your organization. Ask a variety of folks, not just your friends or people who think as you do. Try to engage people at different levels of management as well as non-management employees.

Once you have done that, note the responses from those colleagues in your workbook as your first entry. How did each of them define collaboration? Were they unified in their responses? What do their responses say about the prevailing notions at your firm regarding collaboration? Do those prevailing notions help people work together well or impede them?

AN EXAMPLE OF A TOUGH COLLABORATION CHALLENGE

One of the business leaders I interviewed told me about a tough product development challenge at a company where he previously worked. This company had great success selling an educational electronic toy for children and was anxious to create their next flagship product.

> A cross-functional team was formed to design that next toy. After some research and experimentation, we came up with an idea we felt had a lot of potential. It was presented to the executives, who loved it. So everyone was surprised when the consumer feedback to the prototype was negative.
>
> Mothers felt the product was too expensive. They also felt the wand children used to interface with the toy looked too much like a gun. And they shared several other dissatisfactions. Despite this feedback, the executives felt the toy had much potential. We spent much time reconfiguring the wand. Disappointingly, the next round of consumer feedback remained negative.
>
> Serious conversations were held, but management was still convinced the concept could work. The team made more adjustments and even brought in a consultant. The negative feedback continued. Eventually, we realized there was a bigger problem: The executives had been so vested in making the toy work that they hadn't heard moms say the product was not worth the price. Tough conversations were held, the product was killed, and the company moved on. This process consumed two years.

HOW IT MIGHT HAVE HAPPENED

Great workplace collaborations sometimes result in that next amazing product. At other times, success is realizing that a certain direction isn't working and persuading the team to move in a new direction. The executives at this toy company conveyed that the team's only job was to make this toy successful. The leaders called the shots. The team felt it wasn't their place to convince the executives that the price for the toy couldn't work—until it became painfully obvious.

Picture that design team reacting very differently to the first set of negative consumer feedback. What if they had been empowered and had grasped that the consumers' objection to the price was an insurmountable problem? A basic philosophy of this company had always been to pack as many learning features as possible into every toy. That viewpoint had worked well in the past and it guided this design process. But packing a large number of educational features into this particular toy had raised the price beyond what consumers were willing to pay.

If the team had felt empowered to step back, they could have figured out which features would most appeal to parents. From that, they could have created a toy that was more likely to produce a reasonable profit for the company at a price that consumers were willing to pay. Then, they might have created the next blockbuster. Improving the effectiveness of collaboration at your company increases the chance that you may come up with better ideas and more sound solutions than they were able to at this toy company.

Now, let's explore how companies in vastly different industries make use of collaboration.

COLLABORATION HELPS ACHIEVE GOALS IN EVERY INDUSTRY

Many people believe that the industry your company is in determines whether collaboration is a useful tool for you. That actually is not the case. Regardless of your industry, there are areas where employee collaboration can help you achieve your goals even better. As you read about these three groupings of industries, locate your company in one of them.

INDUSTRIES WITH HIGH NEED FOR CONTROL

Some companies produce products and services that must meet strict safety standards. Most of those companies are in highly regulated industries. They need to do things in certain ways. There is oversight to ensure that things are done in those ways. Examples of such organizations include hospitals, nuclear power plants, and companies producing pharmaceuticals, airplanes, automobiles, and other products for which precision is critical.

Some believe that with those mandates there is no room for employee collaboration. That isn't the case, however. It is beneficial to bring employees together even in organizations that need strong centralized control.

For instance, in the pharmaceutical industry, drug manufacturing requires a high degree of control and standardization. Yet, there are still many areas in pharmaceutical firms in which collaboration greatly increases effectiveness. Think of a drug being tested for effectiveness with a certain group of patients. If a potentially dangerous side-effect is identified, wouldn't you rather have a whole team of scientists and doctors with relevant expertise working together to assess the situation and improve the drug? That's usually how it's done. It's a great example of the value of collaboration in highly regulated industries.

INDUSTRIES NEEDING MODERATE CONTROL

The second group of industries are those that exert moderate control over how work is accomplished. In some of these firms, centralized processes are mandated to protect consumers just as they are in highly controlled industries. Examples of industries with a moderate degree of control include finance, utilities, telecommunications, and some retail firms in food and other areas.

It is easy to understand the need for moderate levels of control in banks or utility companies. In other companies, however, that moderate control is not a result of mandates. Rather, executives have realized that their companies will be most effective with some standardization to help provide products at the quality their customers demand. An example is the Cheesecake Factory restaurant chain. It represents a growing category of businesses catering to higher-end customers that are successfully combining some standardized practices while still retaining some flexibility for employee collaboration and decision-making.

As of a few years ago, that restaurant chain had 160 restaurants, with more than 300 dinner items on the menu (with food choices ranging from pizza to beet salad to miso salmon). Most locations are packed at meal times, evidence of the 80 million customers served annually. Much of the food is shipped from abroad in large quantity, but it doesn't taste like it is mass produced, because it isn't.

The kitchens are the same and food is prepared the same way from location to location. Things are highly computerized, with touch screens for the cook to view the customer order, recipes related to that order, and a timer to let them know when the dish is ready. Despite that standardization, many details are left to the cook's judgment, and special requests are happily accommodated. There is plenty of room for collaboration in areas like the creation of new entrées or tweaking the recipes of existing dishes.[6]

The Cheesecake Factory is just one great example of a large company that has successfully combined standardization with customization, employee involvement, and collaboration. This benefits the customer with high-quality meals that meet their expectations. And it benefits the company with higher profits and satisfied employees. It is a model that more and more companies in this middle group are taking advantage of.

INDUSTRIES WITH THE MOST FLEXIBILITY

There is a third group of industries whose products allow high levels of creativity in both idea creation and production. Strict levels of precision and consumer protection are not needed to guide employees at these companies. Such industries include clothing, furniture, household products, electronic products, and software manufacturers. Products in some of these industries appeal to customers for a short time, after which customers want something new. That translates into a continual quest for new ideas that can be turned into products. It is relatively easy to see how such companies can benefit from collaboration.

Collaboration is a useful tool for companies in all of these three industry groups (high, moderate, and low control). Successful firms bring employees together when it adds value. They may have their employees collaborate in different degrees and manners, but they all do it.

 APPLICATION

Is your firm in a highly controlled industry? One with moderate controls? Or an industry with few controls? Do your leaders define collaboration so narrowly that it limits them from fully seeing some of its uses at your company?

THREE DIFFERENT WAYS OF COLLABORATING

Hopefully, the previous section helped you think of new ways that collaboration can make your company more successful while still respecting the need for standardization and centralized decision-making. Now, let's look at the different ways that employees can work together.

There are many different ways of collaborating. Essentially, all of those variations boil down to three major types of employees working together. Part of the variation between those three types is the amount of freedom employees have to decide when, how, and with whom they will collaborate, and for what length of time.

1. **Task-Specific Collaboration:** In this type, work takes place among a few individuals, hand-selected for their expertise and their ability to contribute to that particular subject. They come together to work on a specific task. Once it is completed, they return to their primary work.

This type of collaboration is the most controlled and narrow in scope. Employee freedom to determine when and for how long that joint work will occur is limited.

2. **Tenacious Team:** This type of collaboration takes place within a team that has a special synergy. That synergy enables them to achieve things they couldn't otherwise accomplish. They solve problems that others thought were unsolvable. They come up with new ideas or modify products.

   This second type of collaboration is less controlled than the first. Members have more freedom to determine when to come together with coworkers. But boundaries do still exist. Because interaction is between members of the same team, it decreases the likelihood of employees losing focus on their day-to-day work.

   Most people think such teams are pretty rare. Further, they sometimes assume that these teams are the result of kismet, and it's impossible to consciously create this kind of synergy. Because of this belief, leaders often try to keep these special teams together indefinitely once they spring up. (One of the goals of this book is to demystify these teams and increase their occurrence.)

   One example of a result of this second type of collaboration is Apple's HomePod. This is Apple's version of a home device that responds to voice commands. Apple's product was not the first or second offered in this niche. They entered this market later, bringing together a highly functioning collaboration to create their own distinctive twist on the product. Whereas other devices emphasize responding to household commands, Apple's device emphasizes its superior sound quality. That modification differentiated their product and allowed them to successfully enter a consumer market that was new for them.[7]

3. **Inclusive Collaboration:** This type of collaboration is the least controlled. Everyone is encouraged to work with others when it's appropriate and can add value. Staff

are seen as valuable contributors within their sphere of expertise. Employees are willing to pause their own work to assist others because the larger goals of the organization are the highest priority.

In this third type, people are more empowered to determine when they can benefit from or contribute to the efforts of others. Employees often contact each other on their own without going through management.

Some leaders are concerned that this third type of collaboration may pull employees off the work that is highest priority and result in missed deadlines. Companies that help employees understand overall company goals and how their work contributes to those goals are not concerned. Setting that context enables employees to make better decisions regarding their work and how much time they spend helping others.

Successful companies in all three groupings (high, moderate, and low control) use all three types of collaboration. The specific needs of the situation determine which type of collaboration is necessary. That is certainly the case among the Silicon Valley leaders I spoke with. They see the value in each of these types of collaboration for different situations.

LINKAGES ACROSS THE ORGANIZATION

It might be helpful to think of your company as a jigsaw puzzle. The work of any team is like one piece in that puzzle. Each of those pieces (or teams) touches four or five other pieces (or teams). Most of us realize that we need to collaborate closely with teams that are adjacent to ours. It may surprise us to realize that we also need to work with teams that are farther away, when those teams affect how the whole puzzle fits together.

Let's return to the Silicon Valley leaders I interviewed. They realize the interconnected nature of work between teams. When asked how important collaboration is at their firms, they said:

- "It's absolutely critical. Because of the nature of our business we *have to* work together to make things happen. . . . We have to have seamless handoffs. Silos don't work here." (Silos are the figurative walls that are built when groups consider themselves autonomous and don't think they need to share information or work with others.)
- "It's critical here; second only to booking income. The things we're creating and solving are complicated. We have to agree on what we're doing, how we are doing it, and whether we are achieving it."
- "One person cannot anticipate all the issues around them. Collaboration is vital."
- "It's essential for knowledge workers. It's the only way we can scale and function at the velocity and pace that we're currently at."

 APPLICATION

As you read how vital collaboration is to these Silicon Valley leaders, what was your reaction? Go out and ask several people: How important do they personally think collaboration is to your company's success? Do they think most people in the company share their perceptions? You may hear a range of responses. Some might say that "employees prefer to be left alone to do their jobs." Others might say that "employees see the value of working closely with colleagues in their own team." Still others may say that "most employees see the value in having others to bounce things off of."

What are these responses cumulatively saying about your company? Does your culture reinforce that collaboration is important to your company's success? Or does it reinforce the notion that collaboration is painful and needs to be limited as much as possible?

Does your company tend to use one or two types of collaboration more than the others (the three types being task-specific, tenacious teams, and inclusive collaboration)? Or do you use all three? Again, note your observations and findings in your workbook.

In Chapter 2, I will talk about important characteristics that collaborators share. It may surprise you to hear that that such a diverse group of people have key philosophies in common, but they do, and these characteristics contribute to the success of collaboration.

②

CHARACTERISTICS OF SILICON VALLEY COLLABORATORS

I have found that many of the Silicon Valley employees who are committed to collaboration are distinguished by six fundamental characteristics:

1. A drive to succeed.
2. The desire to contribute to something meaningful.
3. Persistence.
4. Acceptance of differences.
5. Desire for genuine communication.
6. Connection to company-wide goals.

Let's explore each of them.

A DRIVE TO SUCCEED

The desire to succeed is intrinsic to many Silicon Valley employees. Of course, success means different things to different people. To one

...rson it might mean being inducted into the National Society of Professional Engineers. To another it may be attaining a vice president–level position. Many relate success to financial achievement. Yet there's a common thread. These employees all have an inner drive that pushes them to accomplish whatever success means to them.

Regardless of their job title, these people are willing to work unusually hard—harder than most—to achieve the success they crave. For some, it means discovering some new consumer desire and creating a business around it. For others, it means working at a company that encourages creativity and involves them in developing new products, because not everyone in Silicon Valley wants to start their own firm.

In summarizing a particularly tough project, one Silicon Valley leader said, "We were very proud of what we achieved, but weren't totally satisfied." I asked what he meant by that seeming contradiction. He explained that even when projects are profoundly successful, his company urges employees to look critically at their work and figure out how to do even better with the next project. He likes that. It encourages him to do the best he can, every time. This is just one example of the many ways that Silicon Valley firms encourage employees to tap into their innate desire to be as successful as they can.

THE DESIRE TO CONTRIBUTE TO SOMETHING MEANINGFUL

Every Silicon Valley employee I spoke with told me that they are driven to contribute to something that will make people's lives better. The definition of "meaningful" is as personalized as the desire to succeed. To one person it means curing cystic fibrosis. To another it is helping to develop a smart phone with an earth-shattering new feature. However it's defined, the shared characteristic is a desire to be involved with work that makes a positive difference for people.

One leader said, "We want to know that what we're doing has a purpose beyond profit. Nobody wants to come to work every day and work so hard just to make money." When employees are passionate about what they are creating and the good it will do in the world, they focus on that goal rather than daydreaming about their next vacation.

This was confirmed by Dr. John Sullivan, an internationally known human resources thought-leader from the Silicon Valley, who conducted research at Apple and Facebook. He learned that "The number-one attraction and retention tool at both firms was not the free transportation or food but instead . . . was to have their work impact the world."[1]

PERSISTENCE

The third shared characteristic of Silicon Valley employees is a willingness to see their work as a mystery to be solved. These people see problems and barriers as fun challenges. Their curiosity and persistence energizes them to keep working on an issue to find the best solution while still respecting time and other constraints.

One Silicon Valley leader told of a time when his project team was asked to find the cause of a bug that was making a software program freeze up. They divided the code and each member scoured their section over and over to locate the problem. They couldn't find it. Eventually, the leaders told them to give up and just remove that feature. But they didn't want to. They knew how much customers wanted that aspect of the product. They kept going, working evenings and weekends. And they were rewarded. They felt huge pleasure of accomplishment when they located and fixed the bug.

Employees with this characteristic remind me of Sherlock Holmes. They enjoy using detective-like skills to come up with amazing insights and solutions. Part of their success is based on a willingness to question legacy or sacred cows when they inhibit effectiveness in particular situations.

ACCEPTANCE OF DIFFERENCES

The fourth characteristic these people have in common is a willingness to accept many others as equals. Silicon Valley employees do a very good job of judging others based on knowledge, skills, and contributions. Their trust and respect for someone increases the more that person demonstrates these abilities. These employees are better at refusing to judge people on characteristics unrelated to their job performance (factors such as sexual orientation and nationality).

In many other companies the fact that someone is older, younger, or gay takes precedence over work performance. It shouldn't. These people have to work harder to get respect. Judgments are made based on factors unrelated to that person's competence and performance.

Although Silicon Valley firms are farther along than some other companies in accepting many of these differences, it needs to be explicitly stated that their cultures are not yet inclusive of all people. Progress in Silicon Valley is still limited when it comes to hiring, retaining, and promoting women and people of certain ethnicities. There have been many efforts and some improvement. Success, however, is still a goal rather than a reality for women and some people of color.

That said, Silicon Valley employees are much more accepting of differences than many others. What does this mean for collaboration? Employees are willing to embrace differences rather than shy away from them. They are also willing to embrace out-of-the-box thinking and ideas that others bring to the table.

One Silicon Valley consultant who works with companies in this region said: "When you put a baseball team on the field, you don't put nine catchers out there. You would never win with that strategy. You have to leverage the differences that folks bring." She explained that folks are getting much better at figuring out what skills are needed and disregarding facets of staff unrelated to those competencies. "It is increasingly about skills and competencies rather than the differences that used to (artificially) separate us from each other."

DESIRE FOR GENUINE COMMUNICATION

The fifth characteristic of Silicon Valley collaborators is authentic communication. Those with a Silicon Valley outlook desire genuine conversations in which people can express their views honestly, even when they disagree. Discussions stress directness, straight-talk, and respectful disagreement about content rather than personal attacks.

People are more willing to explore the assumptions beneath their own beliefs without getting defensive. Respect seems both a cause and an effect of these dialogues. It is a cause because people abide by a basic level of civility, and it is an effect as these conversations further build people's regard for others.

CONNECTION TO COMPANY-WIDE GOALS

The sixth shared characteristic is having an awareness of company-wide directions. Silicon Valley employees in firms that stress collaboration are aware of overall goals and how their projects contribute to those goals.

Leaders in many companies try to assign employees to projects that they are passionate about. That passion makes the project more fun, makes employees more vested in its success, and increases their willingness to work harder to achieve it. One of the unintended side-effects, however, is that this passion often makes it difficult for employees to let go of the hard work they've put into the project if conditions change and the work needs to be set aside. In many companies, employees feel betrayed when they have poured huge amounts of energy into a project and it has to be discontinued.

Silicon Valley employees "get the bigger picture" and see themselves as owners of those bigger goals. As a result, they are willing to change direction even when it means dropping something they have put a lot of work into.

SAN FRANCISCO'S UNIQUE HISTORY

Why are these characteristics found in such large numbers in Silicon Valley employees? I discovered that many of these traits have been a part of the culture of the San Francisco Bay area long before the formation of Silicon Valley. Some go as far back as the gold rush of the 1850s.

The San Francisco Bay area became a highly desirable destination after the discovery of gold in 1848. According to the U.S. Census, the population of San Francisco exploded from a mere 200 in 1846 to 34,000 in 1852.[2] The area drew massive numbers of people who planned to mine their way to riches. It also drew another type of entrepreneur. It attracted people who saw even greater potential in creating businesses that would help those miners pursue their dreams.

Those early business leaders had a drive to succeed and a willingness to work hard in pursuit of that goal. A few examples follow, showing how those leaders embodied many of the six characteristics.

Isidore Boudin came from a family of master bakers in France. He brought his family's expertise to northern California in 1849 and started a business baking his now widely regarded bread. It became popular because of its unique taste and texture. Isidore and his wife worked extremely hard to make their business successful. After his death, his wife and daughter continued that tradition. Boudin's sourdough bread is still synonymous with the city of San Francisco. It has the privilege of boasting that it is San Francisco's oldest continuously operating business.[3]

Levi Strauss emigrated from Bavaria in 1846, joining his two older brothers who were already in New York City running a wholesale dry goods business. Levi brought the family trade to San Francisco in 1853 to make his fortune during the gold rush. He split off from his brothers' business and started his own company that produced durable trousers for men engaged in physical labor. Eventually, he partnered with a customer in Nevada to apply a new process that made the pants last even longer. That marked the birth of blue jeans. From those beginnings, Levi Strauss & Co. grew to become the largest pants manufacturer in the country. Mr. Strauss was also very philanthropic, contributing to the betterment of the community and its people.[4]

In 1850, 14-year-old James Folger migrated to San Francisco with his two brothers after a fire destroyed their livelihood in Massachusetts. Upon arriving in this exciting west coast city, his brothers left for the gold mines and he got a job with the Pioneer Steam Coffee and Spice Mills. His hard work resulted in a partnership in the company four years later. Things went well until the Civil

War, when disruptions to the economy forced the business into bankruptcy. But James persevered, paying off the debts and buying out his other partners. Finally, he was free to run the business as he saw fit. He created a special technique for taste-testing the beans, which resulted in better tasting and smelling coffee. Just before he passed away in 1889 he wrote a letter to his son, urging him to remember that reputation is far more important than profit.[5]

These businesspeople are just a few of the many examples of figures who displayed characteristics discussed in this chapter: the strong drive to succeed, a desire to contribute to something meaningful, and persistence.

The fourth characteristic, acceptance of differences, is also a defining characteristic of the San Francisco Bay area. The region has long welcomed individuals and groups who differ from predominant norms. Many people were attracted to this area during the gold rush because of its openness to those with fewer ties to religion and other traditions.

Along with Greenwich Village in New York City, San Francisco became a hub of the Beatnik movement in the 1940s and 1950s. The Beat era appealed to a group of people in their 20s who didn't fit into the middle-class, suburban values that were predominant in this country. Lawrence Ferlinghetti was typical of the people drawn to the Beat movement. He wrote a number of popular books, and founded City Lights Booksellers in San Francisco in 1953. City Lights became a haven in that Beat movement, and still thrives today.

San Francisco was again prominent in the societal changes of the 1960s. Because of that spirit of openness, Hippies were drawn to the city in large numbers. In the 1970s San Francisco became the center of the gay and lesbian rights movement. The Castro grew into an urban gay village. The same decade also saw the election of several openly gay politicians.[6]

This history of accepting differences, started with the gold rush and continued with the Beat, Hippie, and LGBT movements. It is woven into the fabric of Silicon Valley. It encourages evaluating others based on their competencies rather than facets that have nothing to do with their skills. That acceptance of differences, though still a "work in progress," fosters a workplace environment in which people are more accountable for their work and employees are more open to others' ideas.

BEYOND SILICON VALLEY

Many of these characteristics are part of the hiring and training programs at Silicon Valley companies. They are also integrated into employee performance reviews and promotion processes.

Fortunately, none of these six are restricted to San Francisco or Silicon Valley. None are prevented from blossoming elsewhere. These characteristics are found in individuals and companies throughout the world. These outlooks predispose people to work hard to succeed, and work with others to achieve that success.

Because they are such important precursors to effective collaboration, I recommend that you do what you can to help make these six characteristics part of recruiting, hiring, and reward strategies in your company. How can you do accomplish this? There is not a cookie-cutter approach that requires you to do this in any one way. It needs to be synchronous with company values and practices. (Later in the book I will offer ways you can increase your impact on collaboration in your company.)

 APPLICATION

How many of these six characteristics are included in your company's core competencies that are used for hiring, training, and promoting employees? Do staff who are interviewing people for jobs gauge whether candidates have a drive to succeed? Do they gauge whether they consider challenges as fun mysteries to be solved? Do any of these six characteristics show up on employee performance reviews? Does your company conduct employee training to increase genuine communication or connect team projects to company-wide goals?

CORE BELIEFS

Everyone from Henry Ford to Shakespeare has been credited with saying, "Whether you think you can or think you can't, you're right." If you think you can achieve more when you work with others, chances are you will thrive in an environment where collaboration is fostered. If you think you can't, well . . . then that will be true. In other words, our core beliefs about collaboration determine how effective we will be in working with others.

In conducting my research in Silicon Valley, in addition to the six characteristics I also found that employees consistently demonstrate the following five core beliefs:

1. **Some projects need assistance from others.** There are many projects for which I don't have the knowledge to do it all by myself. At times like this, the work benefits from pooling our intelligence. Sometimes I have the expertise but not enough time. At those times it also makes sense to join with others.

2. **Group successes are gratifying in a different way than individual work.** I get personal satisfaction from being part of a successful group project that's different than when I accomplish something on my own. It's incredible to be part of that communal brain.

3. **The chance to learn from others is a chief benefit of collaboration.** When I work with others I learn so much. It's worth it, even if it takes slightly longer.

4. **The chance to teach is another benefit.** I'm happy to share my knowledge with others. It gives me a chance to be in a teaching role.

5. **Collaboration = networking.** By working with and getting to know others, I'm expanding my social network. That network has been valuable to me in the past, and will continue to be in the future.

APPLICATION

Are the five core beliefs prevalent at your company? Or do employees approach joint work with mixed feelings or even foreboding? Your answers will give you clues about how ready individuals in your firm are to collaborate. It is one more piece in the puzzle that will help you improve your company's collaborative practices.

③

STORIES OF SUCCESSFUL COLLABORATIONS

I want to share three stories with you. They were shared with me by Silicon Valley leaders. Each one made some aspects of collaboration come alive for me. I hope they will for you as well.

As you read these, ask yourself, "How does this relate to my company?" Imagine yourself and your coworkers in these situations. Do collaborations like this happen at your organization? If they don't, could you imagine them? (This book will show you how to effect that change.)

CHANGING HOW THE PRODUCT IS DELIVERED TO CUSTOMERS

This first story was shared with me by a mid-level leader at a large multi-national company whose products you probably use on a regular basis. This company delivers an array of products and services to customers. Previously, some of those products were available in physical format and others in digital. Each of those delivery options had limitations.

Leaders were aware of the limitations, but felt they couldn't do anything about them until technology evolved. Those leaders knew that, at some point, changes in technology would make it easier to deliver their products to customers.

Finally, after examining the situation again, the company decided they could finally improve their delivery systems. They knew it would make customers happier. What follows is an excerpt from my interview with the leader about this complex collaborative effort.

> **Leader:** This would be a big change. Employees would need to learn many things to implement the change. Then, customers would need to learn how to perform tasks differently to use the product after the changes were made.
>
> Once some systems were changed, others would need to be altered as well. When we mapped out the interdependencies, we realized that it was massive. We also realized that all the work would need to be completed in a short time frame, about six to eight months from start to finish.
>
> **Me:** Was it going to be difficult to do everything within this timeline? Did that cause additional stress?
>
> **Leader:** It might seem like a daunting task to some companies, but we've made changes in the past that were just as monumental. So we knew we could do it. It's an example of how our culture shines. Once we make a decision, we operate more flexibly and effectively than other companies in which I've worked. I'm really proud of the way we can accomplish huge projects like this so successfully and with such agility.
>
> **Me:** What about your culture allows that flexibility?
>
> **Leader:** We pause and discuss the decision with the employees who need to help implement it. We set the context by sharing as much data and background as we can. We trust our employees and are transparent with what we share. We not only allow, but encourage staff to raise questions, debate the topic with us, and poke and prod.

This helps us to check and make sure we are making the right decisions and considering all the details.

Other companies tend to have one-way discussions. They announce the change and shut the conversation down pretty quickly. We let discussions go on long enough to examine issues and get employee buy-in. Once the discussions are successful, then staff jump into action. They figure out what they need to do and start doing it.

Me: Does that mean you don't have a project management framework that you put in place to help guide a change like this? That everyone just starts working on their part? It seems like that could result in chaos.

Leader: We do have a project management template. But we use it flexibly. We don't adhere to it if it keeps us from doing the right things or creates unneeded bureaucracy. There are levels of project management that have to happen with a complex project like this one.

What I meant when I said employees just jump in, is that most of our staff are quite advanced in their field (we tend to hire senior folks). They are sophisticated and self-starting. They know what's needed of them or know how to figure it out quickly. They jump into action and remain in action, doing their part.

That means we don't have the high overhead that comes with having a lot of middle-managers walking around checking to make sure things are getting done. Folks don't wait for status updates or permissions. It's much easier to get things done at this company, both on a daily basis and when we're in the middle of a big project like this.

Me: Do you have self-managed teams?

Leader: No, it would be going too far to say that. Our low ratio of management to individual employees keeps our overhead costs down. It also makes employees more satisfied because they're empowered to make more decisions and work directly with others without going through management.

People help others when it makes sense. Folks would have to work harder if others weren't seeing what needs to be done and pitching in, often when it isn't even part of their job. That's why things don't need to be as top-down managed here.

Me: How well does that work? Do staff usually make the right decisions?

Leader: Usually, yes. That goes back to leaders setting the context. When we do our jobs well employees can make the right trade-offs.

Me: What did this project mean for other work those employees were doing? Were the employees assigned to this work in between projects? Or were folks reassigned from other work?

Leader: We look for the staff with the right expertise to do a job. The employees did have other work they were doing. Some of the things they were working on didn't have strict deadlines. That work could be re-prioritized and temporarily put aside.

Other folks did have time-sensitive work. They had to work harder to accomplish everything. That's also part of our culture, though. People are willing to put in the extra energy when needed. Part of the reason they're willing to do this is because we don't have a set number of vacation days. Staff know that when the project is done, they can take some time off if they are doing double-duty and working really hard.

Me: Do you find that any employees abuse that open vacation policy?

Leader: No, I haven't found that in my groups or in other groups. People are passionate about working here. They like this culture and like that they're treated as adults. They don't take advantage of it. I've heard the opposite from people in other companies. In competitive cultures, people worry that it's a way to get folks to forgo their vacation because they're afraid they'll lose ground if they take days off. That's not the case here. People are encouraged to take vacation because we know that it refreshes them. Work-life balance is important here. (You will read more about incentives that encourage collaboration in Chapter 11.)

Me: From your perspective was this project a success?

Leader: It was a total success. It was completed within the six-to-eight-month deadline. There was structure to guide the project, but just enough to organize things without constraining staff or making them slaves of the structure. Staff quickly determined what they needed to do and worked together to accomplish it. They worked hard and were fine doing that because they knew they could take a break when the project was completed.

THE TAKE AWAY

This was a complex project that was important to the company. It involved a lot of staff from different groups. It was sponsored by executive leadership, but not micro-managed by them or by mid-level managers. Because of the strong collaboration culture and "get it done" values of this company, this project was successful with a more grassroots, informal approach.

The tight timelines for this big project meant that some employees could re-prioritize and set aside their current work. Others had to re-organize their work and their work-life balance because work couldn't be put on hold. In the end, the project was a great success and didn't seem to put undue strain on employees.

APPLICATION

Do projects run like this at your company? Do your leaders have in-depth conversations with employees when an important project is started, stopped, or changed? Is employee feedback used to tweak and improve decisions? Is enough context typically provided to get authentic employee buy-in? What is the level of employee empowerment or hands-on involvement of managers during a project at your company? Which aspects of this story might you like to bring to your company and adapt to your culture? How hard would it be? What challenges would have to be overcome?

GRASSROOTS PRODUCT DEVELOPMENT

A mid-level manager relayed this second story to me. It illustrates the unique way that his previous employer encouraged new product ideas to emerge. Similar to the company in the first story, this company is also large and also makes their products available in both physical and digital formats.

The manager told me about an idea he had and how he pursued it. He worked in a central group that managed one of this company's flagship products. The product was available to customers for use on their personal desktop computer, on their tablets, and even on their smart phones and smaller devices.

This was not the case from the start. The product had originally been created for desktop computers. Because it had evolved to those other devices over time, users operated it differently on each. On the desktop, they might press a certain key to perform a function. On their phone, they might have to press a different key to perform that same function. This was confusing and frustrating for customers. This manager understood that frustration and decided to investigate the issue further.

Manager: The different ways of operating this product on different devices was a problem. A lot of complaints made their way to us because our central group worked with all the groups that created the various versions of the product. But we hadn't dedicated resources to fix it yet.

Me: Why hadn't it previously arisen as a priority of your group or some other group to fix?

Manager: There were several reasons. Probably the biggest was this company's culture. Each group had a lot of autonomy to be creative and do their own work. Creating one central way that all versions of this product would work would impose constraints on those groups. That was a bit counter to our culture.

Me: How did you initiate this project? What were your first steps?

Manager: I decided to focus on this issue when I had time that wasn't consumed with high-priority work and deadlines. First, I collected available data to see if it confirmed that this was indeed a problem; that customers found it unpleasant to use our product on different devices.

Me: Was the data definitive?

Manager: Yes. It showed that customers were frustrated. They wanted the operating systems to be the same across the various devices. It didn't prove whether we were losing customers—whether they were frustrated enough to move to a competitor's product because of this glitch. While the data didn't answer all of my questions, I felt it was strong enough to make a business case for working on this project.

Me: What did you do next?

Manager: I engaged in some mini-experiments pretending I was the customer. I tried to get into their minds and determine which of the various ways of performing a certain function was likely to be easiest.

Me: How far did you go with your research? Did you redesign the product in detail before taking your idea to anyone else?

Manager: My intent wasn't to come up with the solution by myself. I was just trying to determine how difficult the task seemed.

Then I wrote a proposal that made the business case and outlined how the changes could be made. I shared it with peers to get their ideas and buy-in. Then, I took the proposal to vice president–level leaders and asked if they'd consider letting us work on it.

Me: I assume you got that approval since this did turn into an actual project, right?

Manager: The VPs liked it enough to let me bring together a group to study the issue further. A small number of staff from design, engineering, research, marketing, and a few other groups came together for a week to flesh out the idea.

The work went well. There was consensus that this was doable and important enough to pursue. We made a strategy presentation to that VP group, including some detail about how we'd go about this work, still at a pretty high level. Once again, that VP group approved it to go to the next step.

Me: Did you start working on the project at this point?

Manager: We weren't quite ready to jump in and start working yet. It was a pretty complex task. Over a several month period, mid-level leaders in the groups that own the versions of this product got together and worked out the process. We also started building stronger alliances between those groups.

Me: Then did work begin once you mapped out the process and strengthened those alliances?

Manager: Not quite yet. One of the unique aspects about this company is that work groups have the authority (to a large extent) to decide what they want to work on. If a new idea arises, like this one, you cannot foist it onto the work groups. You have to convince them to take it on as a project, persuading them of its importance relative to other things they could be working on.

Me: That's quite different than how work is assigned in most companies. How did you persuade those work groups to take it on?

Manager: We took the basic proposal that we used to sell the idea to VPs and added details that would inspire employees in these work groups to want to take it on. We anticipated questions they'd have about this project, and about product features, time estimates, and opportunities for them to learn new things while performing the work. Fortunately, the project was appealing enough and the consumer pain great enough that we were able to interest enough work groups that the project could proceed.

Me: Then you began work?

Manager: Not until we completed one last step. We created a project plan to manage the work. We determined who would do what, how people would work together and communicate. Then we began work.

Me: Was it all smooth sailing from that point until the project was completed? Or did you encounter issues that had to be resolved?

Manager: There were challenges along the way. The way those challenges were faced said a lot about the company culture and why I and so many others loved working there.

Two groups that needed to work closely had different tools and ways of performing the work. Some of those tools conflicted with each other. It hadn't been a problem in the past. But it was now, because the parts they were working on had to fit together. They had to come to an agreement on whose tools and process they would use.

One of the groups was under-staffed and also working on another project. The second group knew what kind of pressure the first group was under. Rather than trying to convince the first group to change their tools, which would have added yet more work to their plates, the second group decided to just adapt to the first group's way of doing things.

Me: That's impressive. Is that rare, or did that sort of thing happen regularly?

Manager: It really did happen regularly. That was one of the things I appreciated about the culture. People wanted to help others. It was in the "genes" of the culture.

Me: When issues arose did groups usually work them out between themselves or did management have to get involved?

Manager: Sometimes management got involved. We had to intervene in this project when there was a kerfuffle about one of the features that operated differently in the different versions. The groups couldn't agree on the best way of doing the task. After a certain amount of going back and forth, they realized they needed management to break the stalemate. I and a few other managers got involved and helped them sort out the details and decide which way to go.

Me: Was there any negativity associated with bringing you in to resolve things?

Manager: Not at all. In general, managers let the teams try to work things out themselves. In this case, we noticed the arguing. But we wanted to give them a chance to resolve it. When they weren't able to do that and called us in, that was fine. They had grappled among themselves long enough to know they weren't going to resolve it easily. It was right that they called us in. There was no resentment on their part and certainly no negative feelings on our part. That's one of management's chief roles in this company.

Me: Are there any other aspects of this project that you would like to share?

Manager: We built in some friendly contests to make things more interesting for the teams while they were working hard to solve tough problems. The team that was first to figure out a great solution to some snarly problem got some kudos. The reward was "bragging rights." It wasn't like the first prize was a new car, second prize was $100, and third prize was that you got fired.

We had tried awarding tangible prizes previously at this company (neither the car nor firing them; more like the $100 gift). But we found that these sorts of prizes caused unhealthy competition and kept groups from collaborating fully. We learned to keep the prize at the level of bragging rights.

Me: Was the project successful?

Manager: Yes. The various versions of the product were successfully combined so the operating systems were the same for users. It was a great idea whose time had come. It enhanced customer satisfaction.

THE TAKE AWAY

Unlike the first story in which the project was initiated by executives, this one was originated by an individual manager. The culture of this company encourages all employees to come up with creative ideas and conduct initial research to determine if those ideas are good enough to warrant further exploration.

After review by higher level leadership, approval may be granted to spend a reasonable amount of time detailing the idea and subjecting it to rigorous critical thinking. If that step pans out, then the idea originators get approval to sell the idea to project teams. Those work teams act as a final gate, using their collective intelligence to further assess the idea's worth. This is unique and highly empowering of employees.

A normal number of challenges arose during the work on this project. Many of them were resolved at the work level. Others required the involvement of management. Leaders were brought in only when needed, and there was no negative stigma associated with it.

 APPLICATION

What processes are typically used at your company to create new products or enhance existing ones? Does your company encourage individuals and teams to spend time coming up with and conducting initial research on ideas that might have potential? What did you think of this company's approach of selling projects to work teams? Might that be useful at your firm? How active a role does management take in managing special projects and ongoing work at your company? Does their role resemble the management at this company?

EVOLVING HOW WORK GETS DONE

The third story was shared with me by a Silicon Valley leader who is now a consultant. He was previously a leader at a large, well-known, and highly respected international financial services company in Silicon Valley. He was in the information technology (IT) group.

This company, like both of the other stories, had a philosophy that employee empowerment and autonomy will inspire staff to invest in and have greater ownership over results. In keeping with that philosophy, their software development groups were allowed to select which technology they used to perform their work. As a result, technologies varied from group to group. This practice caused serious problems, however. It made it difficult for teams to work together and share what they were producing because many of those technologies did not communicate well with each other.

Me: What was the goal of this project? And what was your role?

Leader: The goal was to select the technology that all development groups would use moving forward. That meant consolidating to one tool that would be used by over 1,000 different employees. I was the overall project leader.

Me: How did you come to that role? Were you asked to take it on?

Leader: I volunteered because I felt strongly about the need for it. I knew it wouldn't be an easy project, and also knew that if it was to succeed, whoever led the project would need to roll up their sleeves, become quite involved, and do the right thing every step of the way.

Me: Were you working on it by yourself or with others?

Leader: Because of the number of individuals and teams who would be affected by this change and the criticality of their buy-in, our Chief Information Officer partnered with me to pull together architects and technical leaders from the business units. There was representation of technologists from every business unit. This was to ensure that we examined the potential technologies from their perspectives to meet critical needs. We worked collaboratively to select the singular technology that all the groups would use moving forward.

Me: Was this team empowered to make the final decision and implement it? How did that work?

Leader: We worked together and tested a number of technologies. Fortunately, we reached agreement pretty easily about the one we felt was best for our company. We presented our results and recommendations to the CIO and the executive team and they agreed with our conclusions.

Me: Was it easy from there?

Leader: Not by far. The hardest parts were still ahead of us. We had to figure out how to convince staff that it was right to move to one unified technology. And we had to convince them that the one we selected was the right one. Then, we had to figure out how to implement this change that would significantly affect how 1,000 employees performed their work.

Me: How did you persuade employees that this was the right thing to do?

Leader: We started with top leadership, just below the CIO and other executives who had approved our recommendations. We met with those leaders and had an open dialogue about the need for the unified technology, the benefits that would result, and the specific technology that we had selected. Then, as project leader, I attended staff meetings of each manager who worked for these leaders and then staff meetings of the levels below that, until I had spoken with the 1,000 employees in their respective groups.

I explained the problems it was causing the company to use all these different technologies. That was not a difficult case to make since many of those employees had gotten caught up in problems caused by the conflicting technologies. I reinforced the need to stop wasting time re-inventing the same solutions just because these different technologies did not "talk to each other." I heard their concerns and answered them as candidly as I could.

Me: Were there any parts of those conversations that were particularly difficult?

Leader: One of the hardest parts was that employees felt this might signify a move to overall centralization, which might decrease their autonomy in other areas. Through our dialogues, employees saw they were still going to be partners. Their concerns were heard and they were assured that this was not the beginning of a negative sea-change in the culture.

Me: Once you had persuaded staff, how did you implement the change?

Leader: We decided that current projects could be completed using their current technology. We didn't want to disrupt projects that were already under way. New projects would start with the new technology.

We set up a services team to train employees and assist them through the transition to the new technology. We made it fun by bringing in thought leaders from outside of our company to deliver brown-bag lunchtime talks. We created user groups for programmers to share what they were learning. We recruited programmers who had strong expertise in this new technology to form a tiger team that could be called on by any project in the organization that ran into challenges. We set up an internal information portal that included a directory of every team working in the technology and what they were doing. Every time a new group delivered its first project using the new technology, we held a lunch-and-learn with the whole team on stage, sharing the challenges they'd faced and how they had succeeded.

Me: Was the project successful?

Leader: Yes, It was successfully implemented and all 1,000 software development staff were moved to the singular technology. Over time, the initiative had an unintended and very pleasant effect of spawning a massive social network of employees with advanced skills, reaching out to help others as needed.

THE TAKE AWAY

This change related to an internal system, rather than a customer-facing one or new product offering. Its implementation would change how large numbers of employees performed their work. It was taking freedom from individual teams and imposing a level of standardization.

This project fits between the first two stories in terms of how it originated. It began collaboratively between executives and leaders lower in the organization. Because of the importance of this project and also because of the need for widespread employee buy-in, a cross-departmental group of leaders became involved. That group tested various technological options and determined which would best meet the company's needs. Once that platform was selected, there was still much left to be done.

Leadership knew that projects like this one could negatively affect employee morale and commitment. They respected employees and wanted to engage them in meaty conversations about the change. They took the time to have those conversations face-to-face with the teams. Once those conversations were concluded they wisely realized that their work was still not complete. They planned and implemented a carefully designed training and support program to bring staff to the levels of knowledge and skill required to be comfortable and competent with the new technology.

 APPLICATION

How are projects aimed at changing internal systems carried out at your firm? Are leaders or employees from the affected groups involved in making the change? If that isn't the way things are done at your company, could you imagine it being done that way in certain circumstances? When complex changes like this are implemented at your firm, is time taken for important, context-setting conversations? When such changes are made, is training sufficient to help affected employees feel competent with the new ways of doing things?

THE MANY FORMS OF COLLABORATION

There are significant differences in the ways that these three companies went about making complex changes, and how they encouraged collaboration between employees who were involved in the change. These stories illustrate just a few of the forms that collaboration can take. The leaders shared dozens of other stories with me. If I shared them with you here, you would have glimpsed many other ways that employees can come together effectively. Collaboration is not a prescriptive tool that has to be done one certain way, or that cannot be done in other ways.

That said, there are important similarities between these three vignettes. The patterns that run across the companies in these three situations reveal important factors that create a collaborative organization. Those common factors include:

- A company culture that encourages and reinforces collaboration.
- Leaders who model the value of collaboration through their actions with peers and with employees at all levels.
- Employee incentives that encourage appropriate collaboration.
- Management philosophies and practices that provide oversight, guidance, and coaching while allowing employees to have ownership and significant involvement in the projects.
- Project management templates that help organize and manage complex projects without stifling employees who are doing the work.
- Employees who see the value of collaboration.

These and similar factors form the basis of the Silicon Valley Approach to Collaboration, which will be presented in Chapter 4 and explored in the remainder of this book.

4

THE SILICON VALLEY APPROACH TO COLLABORATION

Think again of that jazz ensemble I told you about in the Introduction. Each musician (for instance, a trumpeter), has to be able to play his or her part superbly. In addition, every musician in a section (for example, the horn section) must coordinate their part with the other members of that section and with the other sections. Finally, the band leader helps bring together the products of those individual musicians and sections into a unified sound.

APTITUDES FOR WORKING WITH OTHERS

The saxophonist, drummer, and other musicians know that when they accept a job as a member of that musical group their role is not just to be a soloist. They are being hired to learn their piece brilliantly and then come together with others and blend their work into a great performance.

We should know the same thing when we accept a job with a company. We are not being hired for a "soloist" position in which we *only* perform work on our own. Instead, we are hired to do our job as an individual at times, and "flip a switch" and blend with colleagues at other times.

Working alone requires a different skill than working with others. We use our expertise, figure out how to perform a task, and apply critical-thinking skills and judgment to make the right decisions and produce the best result. Working with others means we have to let go of being "totally in charge" of our work. We bring our expertise and initial ideas. We intend to meld those ideas with others to come up with the best thinking. We give up the ability to unilaterally decide what to do and how to do it. In return, we gain the diverse expertise of others.

Most of us are taught skills related to our expertise before we take a job with an employer. We have not, necessarily, been trained to work with others. Once employed, we get thrown into situations with other employees and are told to get the task done. We limp through our group work, trying to twist and turn our individual skills to that task. Often, that doesn't work very well.

We need to be taught key skills to make us better at the portions of our jobs that involve collaborating with others. That is the primary goal of this book. In this chapter I will discuss *individual skills*, which we personally use when we are working with others, and *team tools*, which are processes we can apply as a group to meld our individual intelligence into collective intelligence.

In addition to these two skill sets, we also need our company to support us in working with others by maintaining a collaborative culture. Although this is not a set of skills like the first two elements, it is a set of practices that is vital for collaboration to thrive. We'll call this *company practices*.

Together, these three factors—individual skills, team tools, and company practices—are the Building Blocks of Collaboration.

INDIVIDUAL SKILLS

There are fundamental skills and attitudes that individuals need to use to be successful when collaborating with others. They include communicating in ways that others understand and that will engage others, listening for deeper meanings in what others are saying, and respecting and trusting others.

If I do not respect your expertise and your cognitive abilities, then I am not likely to place much value on your thoughts and views. If I don't trust that you are being honest and sharing what you know, or I don't believe you'll deliver the things you say you will, then I am similarly not going to put much stock in the things you say and do. Without mutual respect, trust, openness, and effective communication, we cannot achieve effective collaboration.

These skills and attitudes are table stakes (they are essential; you cannot succeed without them). Because they are central, most of us learned them before we arrived at the workplace. In addition, many companies conduct trainings to enhance employees' abilities in these areas. (I will refer to some of them briefly in other parts of the book because of their importance.)

Beyond those fundamental skills, I want to offer what are likely to be four other skills for you to practice as an individual. These four skills are at the heart of the SVAC.

1. **Being True to Yourself:** Realizing what is important to you as you work with others. Being aware of the values that you hold dear and how can you be true to them. Keeping your biggest goals in mind. Knowing the role your emotions play and how to best manage them.

2. **Being True to Others:** Having a genuine connection with your coworkers—that is, caring about them, being open to them influencing you, and supporting and defending them when they're right.

3. **Being True to the Work:** Working with others to explore and agree on the best ideas and the right work for the project. Recognizing that the best result is far more important than any one person being able to claim the idea as theirs.

4. **Being True to the Company:** Staying focused on company goals and how you can best contribute to them with everything that you do.

THE TAKE AWAY

Though all four of these skills make sense to most of us in abstract terms, in practice we usually focus on one or two of them—the ones that resonate for us the most. In reality, though, the four skills are intertwined. If we are not committed to the success of our coworkers, they will be less likely to support us. In that case, the team will often be divisive and achieve much less. In addition, it is much harder to achieve goals if the staff isn't committed to achieving the best work for the project and the company as a whole.

Considering these four skills in juxtaposition with each other gives us a different perspective. We move *from* just advocating for our own goals or our personal views regarding what is right for this project *to* also considering ideas suggested by our colleagues and especially the needs of the whole company. It allows a level of insight that cannot be attained when we are focused on only one or two of them, and enables us to see things differently and make better decisions. (I will offer details for understanding and using these four skills in chapters 5, 6, and 7.)

TEAM TOOLS

Working with others means organizing and performing our work differently than we do when we are working alone. We need three elements:

1. **A process:** When we are coordinating the activities of a number of people, we need a method to help organize and manage the work.
2. **A shared taxonomy:** When we are working together, we often have different definitions of the project or particular topics within it. We need to articulate subjects clearly and precisely to get people on the same page and focused on the right aspects.
3. **Effective decisions about uncertain futures:** We regularly have to make projections about the future. This is

relatively easy to do in a stable environment. It is much more difficult when we're operating in an environment in which things are changing rapidly. I will offer a tool that can help you make more knowledgeable decisions when the future is uncertain.

Let's take a look at these three Team Tools.

A PROCESS

When more than a few staff members are involved in the work, organizing and guiding them means making things more explicit. For instance, we need to determine:

- ⊙ Who is responsible for doing what work, by which deadlines.
- ⊙ General guides for how staff should communicate and interact with others.
- ⊙ How to document important aspects of the work.

Many people believe that we don't need a process to coordinate our work. They assume that employees will naturally come together and make things happen. This is not always the case, especially in complex projects. As one Silicon Valley leader told me: "The mere fact that you have well-qualified people working together to achieve a project doesn't prevent problems. Having a framework that organizes what people are doing makes it much easier to prevent problems and solve the issues that do come up."

Why don't most companies have a framework that they share with employees when they are starting a new project? There are several reasons, which we will explore in Chapter 8 when I provide you with an excellent process that can help guide a variety of projects. Until you get to that chapter, know that there is an excellent method called *Agile*. It's been used successfully for about 15 years to manage software projects.

There are a few people (myself included) who have realized that Agile can be just as useful to guide virtually any project in organizations, not just software development work. Based on this realization

I have re-purposed Agile from its narrow niche and software lingo into a general project management methodology.

A SHARED TAXONOMY

It is relatively easy to understand a project or a specific topic within a project when we are working alone. If we are unclear, we can ask the person who assigned the work or we can research it on our own. We don't have to worry about creating a definition that a lot of people understand and buy into.

Doing work in groups is a whole different story. We each come to the table with our own internal dictionary and lexicon of meanings. Furthermore, we assume that others share our definitions.

Imagine being in a crowd. Someone suddenly shouts the word *duck*. What would your first reaction be? Would you dive under the nearest table for some protection? Or would you look around to catch a glimpse of Donald? Similarly, if someone mentions the word *head* during a presentation, you depend on context to help you figure out whether she referring to "a leader" or "the uppermost part of the human body."

If these two common words have such different meanings, imagine the miscommunication that can occur when talking about complex topics. It's important to be clear and precise. Articulating things so others can understand them is known as *framing* (which we will explore in Chapter 9).

EFFECTIVE DECISIONS ABOUT UNCERTAIN FUTURES

Our work with others often involves making predictions about what will happen. When we are determining what features to include in the next version of our digital camera we are guessing about the future. It would be great to have a crystal ball that could reveal what our competitors are creating for *their* next version. It would also be wonderful to know what new technological innovations might be just around the corner. Additionally, it would be helpful to know what governmental regulations might be on the horizon.

Most of us just sigh and realize that these factors are unknowable.

Because we cannot know them with certainty we assume it's better not to guestimate what might happen. Or we pretend that we know what things will be like and create a plan around our one best theory. Neither of those two options is particularly useful. However, there is a third option: We could factor in potential changes as possibilities. Using those possibilities, we can arrive at decisions that hold-up much better as we move toward that uncertain future.

As one Silicon Valley interviewee remarked: "We have to throw ourselves into the fray. Ask what is really going on. What is driving this to happen and why? Sometimes the world is not the way I thought it was 12 months ago or even 12 minutes ago. I'm often not able to see that until the group helps me to see it differently." There is a tool that can help us do this in an organized way. It is called *scenario planning*. (I will share it in Chapter 9.)

COMPANY PRACTICES

The individual skills and team tools we've been discussing are building blocks that contribute to effective collaboration. They're available for any of us to use at any time. The third building block is one that we, as individual employees or lower-level managers, have less direct control over. This building block consists of three critical company-level practices that either enhance or inhibit employees' ability to collaborate effectively.

The three practices are *management practices, employee incentives,* and *access to each other*. Because they are crucial to successful collaboration, these three Company Practices are an integral part of this book. Although you cannot enact most of them on your own or just in partnership with other members of your team, you can talk with your management about their importance. (A suggested process for having such a conversation with management will be supplied in Chapter 14.)

MANAGEMENT PRACTICES THAT SUPPORT COLLABORATION

Management is considered both art and science for a reason. At some point, we wisely realized that where human behavior is concerned, it is impossible to manage work and people in a singular way that applies equally well in all circumstances. Back in the early 1900s, when big organizations first came into being, we hadn't realized this yet.

In those early years, more than a century ago, management experts tried to systematize exactly how employees should do their work and how managers should supervise them. It was management's job to create the goals and strategies. It was also their job to determine what work was needed to achieve those goals. Then they delegated that work to specific employees. They told employees exactly how to do their job, and made sure they did their job in those ways (and did nothing else).

At first, that worked reasonably well in the manufacturing industry when most employees were unskilled and worked on the assembly line. It worked less well in industries where the work was less well-defined or where employees were more skilled.

As more and more companies have sprung up in industries that are less well-defined, systematizing employee and managerial behaviors has become increasingly less effective. As a result, the roles of managers in most companies have evolved significantly over the last 50 years. In the wise words of one Silicon Valley leader who worked at a major corporation for many years and now consults internationally: "People don't want to be 'managed.' You can manage a budget. You can manage schedules. You need to lead people."

There are a number of management practices that foster a collaborative environment in which employees want to and are equipped to work with others. This book will identify and discuss those practices. They include: strategies and goals that support collaboration, organizational structure, management philosophies and values, inspiring employees, supervisory practices,and corrective practices. (I will discuss all of them in Chapter 10.)

EMPLOYEE INCENTIVES

It's not that we humans are selfish. Quite the opposite. We prove every day that we care about and want to help others. We willingly assist our friends, neighbors, and coworkers, and are generous to strangers. Experts confirm that we humans are indeed social animals. The majority of us get huge psychological rewards from living and working in groups, and assisting others.[1]

We may not be selfish, but we are self-interested. That is appropriate. We work for many reasons. We have a desire to succeed, a longing to contribute to something meaningful, or a need to achieve something notable. We want the financial rewards. If we feel our compensation may be compromised by working with others, then we are less willing to collaborate.

A company's employee incentive package is a primary mechanism that leaders can use to encourage staff to work well with others. Most companies ignore this opportunity and base their pay package on individual achievements, rather than including team or organizational achievements.

It's easier to determine how much work someone has done on their own than to figure out how to apportion part of an employee's pay to group or whole-company results. But this is one of those cases in which taking the easy route is not the same as taking the effective route. If a company is only rewarding the work employees do by themselves, that's the work that staff will concentrate on doing well. Companies need to base part of their rewards on how well employees do the "group work" portion of their jobs.

There are many different ways to do this. Every company needs to craft financial packages that are right for them. We will explore some of the ways that Silicon Valley companies approach this topic to give you some ideas. In Chapter 11, I will show how Silicon Valley deals with: compensation, bonuses, deferred compensation, vacation policies, and other benefits.

ACCESS TO OTHERS

The final company practice with enormous influence on collaboration is whether employees have easy access to others with whom they need to work. If employees don't have a way to work together it's going to severely limit the effectiveness of collaboration. Wrapped up in the concept of employee access are:

1. Physical office design. Are offices configured in a way that enhances interaction between employees who can most benefit from that interaction?
2. Geographic dispersal. How do people interact with others when they work across the city, across the country, or even across the world?
3. Telecommuting (work-at-home) options. Is remote work an option? If it is, how do employees access others who are not physically present or at another office location equipped with technology that allows them to work together?

These three aspects of employee access are critical. They either contribute to effective collaboration or inhibit it. I will cover them in Chapter 12. You might be surprised by some of the findings in this area.

VISUALIZING THE SILICON VALLEY APPROACH TO COLLABORATION

As the previous sections outlined, the SVAC is comprised of three building blocks: individual skills, team tools, and company practices. This book will teach you tangible skills and tools to help you apply each of these building blocks even more effectively. It's a lot of material. Because it covers a lot, it might help to see it visually. The following graphic brings the SVAC together into a coherent picture.

When you successfully combine these three building blocks, people act differently. They act differently because they value working with others. They act differently because they know it often results in amazing ideas. They act differently because they know their company expects it of them, and will reward them for doing it.

When every employee and manager acts in accord with these areas, then you have built a Collaborative Ethos. That Ethos differentiates the Silicon Valley leaders and their companies from other companies.

Silicon Valley Approach to Collaboration

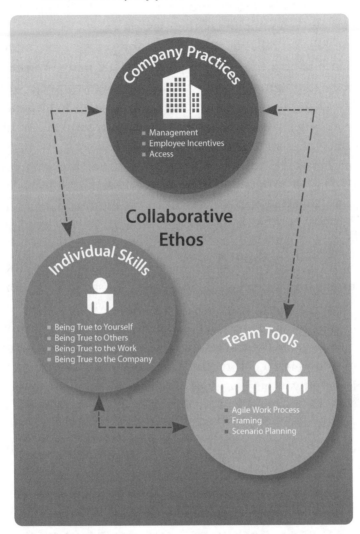

Graphic by Eileen Zornow

It may sound magical; the results certainly can be, but the process is not. It happens when you find people who agree about the philosophy of collaborating, teach them additional skills, give them team tools, and ensure that company practices support and encourage them to work together.

I asked those leaders if they could put into words how they turn a set of very practical tools into the magic of a Collaborative Ethos. What follows is a sampling of their responses.

One Silicon Valley leader with many years of executive level experience explained, "We are pretty unique here. In other organizations, managers and individual employees compete with one another. Here, we are a unified group. We don't vie to be better than our peers. Sure, we want to be the best; and strive to be. As an organization. Not as an individual."

Another leader who worked at less collaborative companies in the past said he realized that "life is too short to stay at the low end of the collaboration scale. If not at the top, then this place is definitely near it. It's not perfect, by any stretch. But there's a different level of trust here. You can take chances, voice your opinion."

A third leader, who has led several successful start-ups, described his current firm's secret as "a willingness to sacrifice ego for intellectual curiosity and excellence." He acknowledged that "there is a healthy amount of ego here, like everywhere. But it is combined with a willingness to be open-minded enough to listen and consider new ideas and not feel threatened."

Now that you have read all about the Silicon Valley Approach, and seen a visual depiction of it, I will offer a virtual tour of one Silicon Valley company whose thinking and practices exude a Collaborative Ethos and mirror the SVAC. I will refer to this company as Superb Software (SuSo) to preserve their anonymity.

SUPERB SOFTWARE: ONE COMPANY THAT PERSONIFIES THE SVAC

Superb Software has colossal goals. They don't want to just succeed a bit more than their competitors. They are making big bold bets. They want to change their whole industry. They see their company as unique and want their employees to feel the same. They run their company with this perspective in mind.

INDIVIDUAL SKILLS FOR WORKING WITH OTHERS

Employees at SuSo live this company's values. Whereas values are nice platitudes at some companies, they are guiding principles at this firm. Those values start with high performance. Then they move to autonomy with responsibility, high pay, context rather than control, and staff who are aligned with their colleagues.

Building from those general principles are a number of behaviors that are expected and rewarded at SuSo. Those behaviors include: 1) making wise decisions; 2) listening well before reacting; 3) accomplishing remarkable things in important areas; 4) learning quickly, broadly, and eagerly; 5) finding practical solutions to hard problems; 6) saying what you think even if it's controversial (and not just saying it, but also doing what's right); 7) inspiring yourself and others on your quest for excellence; 8) being candid and direct; and 9) seeking what is best for the company rather than just yourself or your group.

Superb Software knows how important it is to find employees whose values and behaviors fit the company culture. They know that problems arise when there is a mismatch between individual and organizational values. They believe their culture of high performance attracts staff who thrive on hard work, excellence, candor, and change.

TEAM TOOLS: THEIR THOUGHTS ABOUT HAVING AN ALL-PURPOSE PROCESS

They have thought long and hard about processes and rules at Superb Software. They believe that as companies grow and staff size increases, most firms become too dependent on processes and rules. They understand that most companies craft policies to help employees be more effective and efficient. In their eyes, however, elaborate procedures and rules end up thwarting employee productivity. Contrary to those other companies, leaders feel their success depends on employees having the flexibility to remain creative and the incentive to work hard.

As a result, leaders go out of their way to avoid unnecessary bureaucracy. They also know that they don't want the opposite: chaos. So they work to create a balance. They don't reject all process as some companies do. They believe that having frameworks to guide complex projects is desirable. They work hard to find and use processes that guide employees without unduly restricting them.

Rather than adjusting to complexity, they try their best to minimize it. They feel that keeping things as simple as possible is a better way of helping employees know what to do than establishing burdensome processes. This even affects their products. Their business model is to sell a few big products rather than a lot of small ones.

They do not spend a lot of time looking for efficiencies that restrict how people get things done. They consciously avoid "rule creep" (the way that rules seem to take on a life of their own and increase until they become unmanageable).

It's not that they don't appreciate efficiency. They do. They expect individuals and groups to be highly efficient. They just choose not to back that expectation with long lists of do's and don'ts. Because they don't use a lot of checklists and guidelines, they realize that errors happen. They're okay with this, as long as those errors are discovered and corrected quickly.

It's important that employees learn from each error. If employees make different errors in the future, that's okay as long as the errors are reasonable ones, and as long as they are fixed as soon as possible. They're not okay with the same errors being repeated because folks didn't learn from their mistakes.

COMPANY PRACTICES

MANAGEMENT PRACTICES

SuSo's management values context over control. They believe that providing context (the why) and treating employees as intelligent adults will result in more sound decisions than putting lot of controls in place.

Leaders make sure that employees understand Superb Software's goals and that employees can link their individual and group work to those goals. If employees use faulty reasoning or make bad decisions, leadership feels the responsibility falls more on them than on those individual contributors. They suspect most poor decisions could have been prevented if leaders had provided more context to staff.

Superb Software's management philosophy around collaboration is that groups need to be highly aligned with others with whom they are working. They expect staff to share information that others might need to do their jobs well. Many of their meetings are focused on getting and keeping that alignment. They don't tend to use meetings for one-way information flow. They generally believe that is better done through email or other means.

Leaders encourage behaviors that build trust between employees; behaviors such as going out of one's way to offer assistance to others and not waiting to be asked.

EMPLOYEE INCENTIVES

SuSo strives to hire the best and brightest people. Some firms hire one or two stars and build their teams around those individuals, much in the same way that many sports teams do. Those people have higher status. They get the ear of leaders more often. Other staff are expected to heed and support them. Because Superb Software strives to hire stars in every position, it creates a different kind of team.

There is an explicit expectation that staff will work together and assist others. Hoarding and cutthroat behavior are not only not rewarded, they are not tolerated. Leaders at SuSo encourage employees to help others be great and reward employees who do this.

Whereas "C-grade" (adequate) performance is acceptable at some companies, it is not at this firm. Leaders make it known that "just adequate" performance at this company earns employees an invitation to leave. This does not mean that Superb Software does not believe in loyalty. If a great employee is facing challenges, the company will cut them some slack for a period of time. But not forever.

They don't feel it's fair to ask other employees to carry the load for low-performers indefinitely. In the same way, they would not expect employees to stay with the firm indefinitely if the company gets into financial trouble.

They believe that in companies like theirs, the difference between what really hard workers achieve and what average performers accomplish is enormous. One of the yardsticks managers use to assess employee performance is to ask themselves, "How important is this person to our company's success?" You can answer this question if you understand what that employee is doing.

Performance reviews at Superb Software measure how hard employees work and what they accomplish. Managers do their best to assess employee efforts and results rather than the number of hours they've worked.

The company also assesses how each employee works with others. Some firms only look at bottom-line results and not work relationships. It is important whether those results enhance collaboration and the successes of others.

This company has a philosophy of continuous, honest feedback. They believe that no employee should be surprised by feedback they receive during a formal review. They should have heard that feedback before. Performance feedback is seen as a dialogue. Employees are not only encouraged to ask managers for feedback, they are expected to do so.

SuSo promotes employees only when the group and company need someone in that higher-level position. They believe that other companies use promotions as part of the reward system that indicates to staff that they are doing a great job and valued.

Leaders at this company feel that gives the wrong message. They believe that salary and other benefits should be used to reward employees who do a great job and that promotions should occur only when the organizational requirements indicate it. When a position is opened, people are only considered for promotion when they are a star in their current role and an extraordinary role model for others.

Company policy around salary is simple: They pay at the top of the market for every position, in keeping with their expectation that employees have a drive to succeed and are willing to work very hard. They conduct market surveys annually to determine pay levels for key positions so they can keep paying at the top of that range.

With this philosophy, the company does not give raises and bonuses based on a generic formula. They feel this is a plus because, in their view, generic formulas for annual employee rewards do not tend to have the intended effect at most companies.

SuSo offers benefits that they hope employees will enjoy and that make them feel even better about working there. They offer very good food and have even better offerings at their occasional parties. They try to maintain really nice offices—places that employees want to come to and like spending lots of time at. They do these things in order to attract and retain wonderful employees.

Employees at Superb Software are encouraged to take as much vacation as they feel is appropriate, as long as it fits with the company's needs for their services.

SuSo used to have standard vacation packages. All employees received a certain number of vacation days per year. At some point they realized this policy no longer made sense because employees often work evenings and weekends (at least checking emails), and occasionally take personal time during the work day. When an employee pointed out the contradiction between tracking vacation time but not hours worked, they realized that their policy no longer made sense.

In keeping with this philosophy they did away with the vacation policy that doled out a certain number of days to every employee. They did not do away with their expectation that employees should use their judgment regarding vacation time. They want all employees to take significant vacation time to enjoy life and return to work refreshed and renewed. As with most things, they just ask employees to act in the company's best interest as well as their own.

Superb Software prides itself on continually "trying to get better at seeking excellence." When you see it in its entirety, the policies and practices make sense, fit together well, and are a terrific example of a Collaborative Ethos.

THE TAKE AWAY

You may have noticed the overlap between Superb Software's guiding principles and the Individual Level of the SVAC as well as the six Characteristics of Collaborators. (The four individual skills of Being True to Yourself, to Others, to the Work, and to the Company. The six characteristics of having a drive to succeed, the desire to contribute to something meaningful, persistence, acceptance of differences, desire for genuine communication, and connection to company-wide goals.)

Additionally, SuSo's team tools and company practices largely reflect those of the Silicon Valley Approach to Collaboration.

It's not coincidental that there is such direct overlap between this company's principles and practices and those suggested in this book. The content of this book was not adopted solely from this particular company. In many ways, this company is like the other 27 companies whose leaders shared similar information to help develop this thinking.

The SVAC Model is practical and is being carried out in companies across this region every day.

 APPLICATION

Compare this company to yours. Are there areas of overlap? Do any the ideas shared here raise any possibilities for your company?

With this bigger picture in mind, let's explore the details of the Silicon Valley Approach. Chapter 5 immerses you in the four individual skills that form one of the crucial building blocks of this approach.

5

INDIVIDUAL SKILLS THAT ENHANCE COLLABORATION

Perhaps you have seen that optical illusion that looks like a picture of a woman. When we first look at it, some of us see an old lady. Others see a young woman. A few even see the subtler picture of an elderly man. Once the picture crystalizes for us, it's hard to see the alternatives. We assume that we are seeing the entire picture, but we realize our mistake when someone points out the other two faces. We then marvel at how difficult it was to see the other faces until they were revealed to us.

This exercise reminds us that we continually filter our surroundings and select what we pay attention to. Our brains only process a portion of our visual environment. Then, we organize and interpret what we are seeing in order to make sense of it.

Using the four individual skills together (Being True to Yourself, to Others, to the Work, and to the Company) expands our view and helps us notice more of the crucial stimuli around us. Knowing how to use the four skills is much like seeing the entire picture when it comes to that optical illusion. It can help clear the fog that can surround us when we're in a complex situation.

The following image brings the four perspectives together visually, as they are meant to be used in unison with each other.

Skills for Working with Others:
The 'Being True' Model

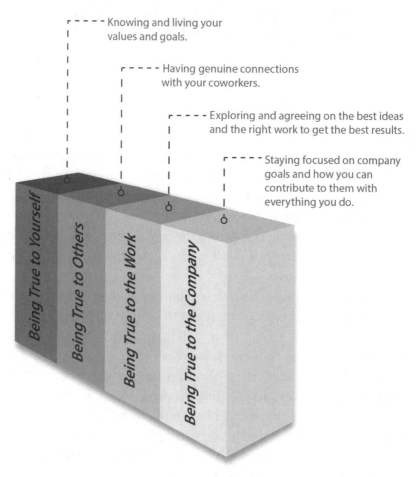

Graphic by Eileen Zornow

The remainder of this chapter will teach you what each of these "being true" skills means. Following those explanations, a case study will illustrate how you can use them to get a clearer perspective on a particular situation. Then, you will have the opportunity to apply these four skills to a current challenge you are facing at your company.

Let's start by exploring what Being True to Yourself really means.

BEING TRUE TO YOURSELF WHILE WORKING WITH OTHERS

When you are Being True to Yourself, you are aware of what is important to you and act in accordance with those beliefs. It means identifying your values and behaving in ways that reflect them. It entails knowing your goals and acting in ways that move you closer to them. It also means being aware of the role your emotions are playing and helping to manage them.

The line from Shakespeare's *Hamlet*, "This above all: to thine own self be true," has intrigued people for centuries. How many other lines, written in the 1600s, would you recognize? For most of us, the number is very few. But this one is memorable.

In delivering the 2005 Stanford Commencement Address, Steve Jobs similarly said: "Your time is limited, so don't waste it living someone else's life. . . . Have the courage to follow your heart and intuition. They somehow already know what you truly want to become."[1]

Both of these geniuses remind us to be honest with ourselves about what's important to us. It's vital to our emotional well-being and our satisfaction with life.

Let's explore the three aspects of Being True to Yourself (values, goals, and managing emotions).

LIVING YOUR VALUES

Being True to Yourself starts with your values, the things you hold dear in life. They explain the decisions you make and the actions you take. If authenticity is one of your chief values, for instance, then you will act in accordance with it by speaking up when something is important to you.

Many experts have studied company values. One expert looked at data regarding company values for a 25-year period. His findings included: "Companies that had very clear written values to which everyone in the company ascribed earned an average of 700 percent greater profit over the 25 years than other companies in the same industries that did not."[2]

Exactly the same holds true when it comes to importance of personal values. In Gandhi's words, "Happiness is when what you think, what you say, and what you do are in harmony."[3]

If you are unaware of your own values, you will not have a North Star guiding you. Without this guiding force, you may act in ways that make you feel uncomfortable, and be unable to figure out why. I encourage you to get clear about your values. (Tips for doing this will be provided in Chapter 6.)

KEEPING YOUR BIGGEST GOALS IN MIND

Being True to Yourself also means having goals and pursuing them. To paraphrase the Cheshire Cat in *Alice in Wonderland*, if we don't know where we want to go then most any road will do.

Some of our goals follow from our values. If taking care of your family is a value of yours, then you may create a goal that encourages you to spend time with them. You might also set a goal related to career success so you can provide for your family financially.

Having explicit goals makes it more likely that we will achieve the things in life that are important to us. Yet, how many of us take the time to figure out our goals? Brian Tracy, an expert in individual and organizational development, estimates that only 3 percent of adults take the time to set realistic goals and create plans to achieve them.[4]

Psychology professor Gail Matthews recently conducted a study on goal-setting. She found that writing down our goals and action plans, sharing them, and updating a friend about our progress, makes a big difference. Among the people who took all those steps, 76 percent of them achieved their goals. Among those who had goals but didn't take any of these other steps, only 43 percent achieved their goals.[5]

If you haven't yet, join that 3 percent. Once you have formulated those goals, commit to and share with a few others who will support you in achieving them. Be truest to the goals that are most important to you. We sometimes lose sight of our big goals in the heat of the moment and later realize that we achieved a smaller goal at the expense of something that's more central to us. (Chapter 6 will offer tips for goal-setting.)

YOUR EMOTIONS

It used to be common for leaders to tell employees to "leave your emotions at the door when you come to work." They implied that we could disconnect our emotions. They also implied that emotions are destructive and inappropriate in the workplace. Neither of those inferences is correct. We experience emotions all the time. We couldn't shut them off if we wanted to.

One study reported that we experience an average of 500 emotions every day and about 3,000 a week. That means we have a whopping 150,000 emotions in an average year.[6] We don't achieve personal success by putting our emotions aside. Nor is it about being perfect. It is about doing the most we can with what we have. It's about allowing our feelings, along with our intellect, to inform us and guide our responses and behaviors appropriately.

Let's create a shared understanding of this concept we call *emotion*. Things happen that cause a reaction in us; those things can occur outside or inside of us. An example of an externally caused feeling might be when your manager lets you know that she was unable to get approval for you to join a project that you really wanted to work on. An example of an internally caused reaction might be if you are mulling over a training course you are taking at work. You feel a knot in the pit of your stomach. You realize that you are totally lost in the class but don't want to admit it in front of your coworkers.

In both of these examples, a part of our brain reacts to what we are experiencing by releasing a burst of chemicals. Dr. Leda Cosmides and Dr. John Tooby, both professors at University of California, explain that this is totally natural. The chemicals (also known as our emotions) cause feelings, sensations, moods, and bodily responses.[7]

At the same time that we are experiencing emotions, another part of our brain is processing our perceptions into cognitive thoughts. But the part of our brain that produces our emotional reactions works faster than the cognitive part of our brain. Because emotions come first and because they are powerful, our emotions influence our thinking.

When we can identify and understand our emotions, we are much less confused by our interactions with others and our internal reactions. When we manage those emotions they assist us. When we do not, they can work against us. Study after study has found that emotional intelligence (EQ) is more important than our IQ or our technical expertise in determining our career success.[8] For this reason as well as many others, it's well worth the effort to manage our emotions.

The term *e-motion* is a great way to describe the effects of those chemical reactions. The feelings and moods that are triggered often linger until we do something (get into "motion") and let go of them. The word *e-motion* reminds us that some energy was created in that reaction and we need to dispel the feelings in a healthy way. If we do not, then we may inadvertently act out those feelings in a way that is bad for us and for others.

Learning to harness our emotions allows us to be more effective at work as well as at home. (Chapter 6 will offer tips for identifying and managing emotions.)

APPLICATION

Are you aware of your values? Do you act in accordance with them? Do you have goals? Do you have action plans to help you achieve them? Have you shared them with others who can help you focus on them? Are you aware of your emotions as they are happening? Are you able to manage those emotions? How might you want to be even truer to yourself moving forward? How might your company better foster a culture where employees are true to themselves?

You now know what is involved in Being True to Yourself. Read on to learn what Being True to Others means.

WHAT BEING TRUE TO OTHERS MEANS

Being True to Others means connecting with them, being open to their influence, and supporting them. It means seeing people with whom you work as part of your network. This does not mean you are best friends with your coworkers, but having a genuine connection with them does change the quality of your work with them. It creates an emotional bond.

As two experts in the field, John Parker and Edward Hackett, have said, "Emotions spark creativity, tighten social bonds, and lower barriers to collaboration."[9] Our emotions act as a social lubricant, creating a connection that inspires great thinking.

Google recently came to a similar conclusion. They wanted to figure out why some of their teams were much better at collaborating than others. They conducted research to find out. They expected to find things they could quantify and share with other teams, like team size and structures for productive work, but instead they found that one of the most influential factors was psychological safety. The teams that made it safe for coworkers to speak up and know they wouldn't be judged poorly were the teams with the most robust collaboration. They found that "Without psychological safety, there's no true collaboration."[10]

Psychological safety happens when people respect others enough to want to listen to them. We tend to be more open to truly hearing what others have to say when we have that connection. One Silicon Valley leader I spoke with talked about the importance of "choosing your words wisely and be willing to forgive. If you're not willing to do that with others, then you can't expect it back from them. We all get mad and express it. That isn't a bad thing in itself. It's how we do it."

Imagine yourself in a project with 12 people who serve a variety of functions in your company. This team has a very important task: to create a new product for teenagers. This will help your company appeal to a new customer group. You've been meeting for seven months, but executives were expecting to receive several potentially great new ideas from the group long before this. Instead, what you have to show for your time and efforts are frazzled nerves and poor relationships.

This is how one of your teammates describes the meetings: "We push our views while resisting others who are pushing theirs. We tend to judge their ideas without evidence, and only look only for data that supports our own views. We don't even hear what others are saying. Instead we wait for them to finish and then go back to our own thought. Or worse, we interrupt others before they even finish what they're saying."

She goes on to quote Thomas Jefferson: "I never saw an instance of one or two disputants convincing the other by argument."[11] She concludes, "Despite the fact that we know this, we persist in trying to persuade others through argument and debate. We talk near each other, or at each other. We don't to talk with each other."

Imagine if your coworker could have described the following process instead. "Conversations between us were shared inquiries. We are able to think together rather than all being in the same room and still thinking alone."[12] "We brought out new ideas; things we never thought before, never-mind having shared with others. We were able to surface alternatives and compare them side-by-side, using our collective experience. It was energizing and exciting to be part of this team." What helped our team work this way? "We achieved this because of the connections we have with others. We took time when we first started working together to get to know each other. That and the bonds we continued to build as we worked together made all the difference in the world."

The first case described employees who were not Being True to Others. The second one described employees who were. Which would you rather have?

 APPLICATION

How do you rate with respect to Being True to Others? Do you consciously create connections with coworkers? Does your company facilitate the creation of connections and emotional bonds? Are employees reinforced for Being True to Others?

WHAT IT MEANS TO BE TRUE TO THE WORK

Being True to the Work means that you are committed to exploring and agreeing on the best ideas and the right work for each project. It means that getting the best result is far more important than any one person being able to claim an idea as theirs.

If people think they have the best answer and their job is to convince others of that fact, then work sessions are going to be discordant. If folks know their knowledge is crucial and that the ultimate solution will combine the best of those ideas, then work sessions are going to be more melodious.

Two key skills can assist you in Being True to the Work: being open to new information and exploring the options.

BEING OPEN TO NEW INFORMATION

We all have "spheres of knowledge." However, we often don't see the limits or edges of our knowledge until we stumble on them. When we discuss something with others, we realize that we have stepped into an area in which we are less certain. Suddenly, we are conjecturing rather than knowing. Ideally, that fuels our desire to learn. We open ourselves to learning when we expand our skills in: noticing what we are seeing, scanning for relevant details, using our senses to take in information, and seeing the patterns in information. (I will offer tips for doing this effectively in Chapter 7.)

EXPLORING THE OPTIONS

Making the right decisions about both details and big-picture issues is trickier when we are working with others. It means doing work beforehand so we arrive at the meeting ready to contribute. And it means setting our initial conclusions to the side for a bit, so everyone can now see and analyze options from different perspectives. It means seeing the whole picture (seeing the young woman, the old woman, *and* the old man, simultaneously). There are team tools that can help you see these multiple perspectives and bring out the group's collective intelligence. (Chapter 7 offers two important tools for doing this.)

 APPLICATION

Do leaders reward employees for Being True to the Work? How would you rate your openness to new information and to learning? Does your company have tools that help groups explore options and to come to the best possible conclusions? Are trainings offered to teach these skills?

BEING TRUE TO THE COMPANY

Being True to the Company means staying focused on company goals and determining how you can contribute to them. Your ability to do this depends on having an astute awareness about your company and the directions it is taking. It means you understand the organization's goals and what you and others need to do to help reach them.

In the words of Abraham Lincoln, "Commitment is what transforms a promise into reality."[13] When we are committed, we do things because we feel ownership rather than just responding to a request. Commitment and ownership happen when we are passionate about what we're doing and want it to succeed. They happen when we are intellectually and emotionally bonded to the work, the people, and the organization. Those bonds don't just occur merely because we work at a company and get a paycheck. They occur when we are treated as vital contributors.

LEADERSHIP'S ROLE IN HELPING EMPLOYEES BE TRUE TO THE COMPANY

Your company's leaders have a big part in creating a culture in which you want to be and can be true to the company. People can't help your company reach its goals if they are not privy to the information that enables them to make great decisions. Leaders in collaborative organizations continually share information with staff and provide them enough context to enable them to understand it.

Let's explore how this is done at Facebook. "Unlike [other] tech companies . . . which keep employees in the dark about projects and ambitions, Facebook routinely shares all kinds of secrets with all of its workers."[14]

Mark Zuckerberg and other leaders at Facebook share confidential and proprietary information openly with staff (including company strategy, directions, and much more). That information doesn't make its way out of the company inappropriately. Why? Because Mark has a strong pact of trust with staff. He makes it known when the information he is sharing is confidential, and that he trusts staff to keep it in-house. People are treated as adults and expected to act that way.

This is not to say that every company can or should be totally open about everything. Any company establishing a Collaborative Ethos needs to determine how open they can be with employees on any given subject, and then share with them accordingly.

EMPLOYEE'S ROLE

Once leaders share with employees, it is up to staff to use that information appropriately to make better decisions so they can have a bigger impact.

When big-picture directions change and leaders have shared the context of those changes, employees need to be willing to let go of projects, even the ones that they're excited about, if they no longer fit into the bigger picture. It's much easier to accept the challenge of letting go of work folks were passionate about when they understand the need to do so. (I will share tips in these regards in Chapter 7.)

 APPLICATION

Do leaders enable employees to be true to the company by sharing information and setting context? Does your company have a culture in which employees feel commitment and ownership? Do employees understand the trust inherent in that sharing, safeguard private information, and do the right things with it?

SEEING THESE INDIVIDUAL SKILLS IN ACTION

This case study will show you the four individual skills in action. Imagine that you are a market research director at a company that sells pet accessories. Among your company's bread-and-butter products are dog and cat collars. You offer a variety of collars and they account for a good chunk of your business.

Recently, an inventor approached your company with a product innovation. Using her device, customers can design their own collars by making choices from a list of offerings, such as color, width, and fabric. Your executives ask you to conduct some market research to determine whether consumers will like this product and if they would be willing to pay the additional cost that your company would have to charge for it.

You set up some market tests to help answer this question. The results of your research show that consumers prefer existing pet collars at the lower cost.

That creates a dilemma. You know that, though market research data is extremely valuable, there are times when it doesn't tell the whole story. This is especially true when the new product is so unlike the current one that it's hard for people to conceptualize. You believe this may be one of those times. You feel conflicted, so you decide to use the four individual skills to help you decide what to do.

MARKET RESEARCH DIRECTOR: BEING TRUE TO YOURSELF

What does Being True to Yourself mean when it comes to this business opportunity? You suspect that the results of this study were likely skewed because consumers couldn't envision how the new collars would be better than existing ones. If you're right about this, then you should counter these results and recommend that your company buy this innovative process.

But taking this action could undercut the credibility of your research moving forward. Others may question whether your data should be ignored if they disagree with future results. In that sense, Being True to Yourself might mean preserving your credibility. In that case, you might want to recommend not pursing this product. But your gut tells you this is not the right answer. Before you decide which way to proceed, the model asks you to consider all four skills. So you move on to the second one.

BEING TRUE TO OTHERS

When you pause to think about what Being True to Others means, you remember that one of your peers on the team exploring this product is an engineer who spoke up against the new collars in earlier conversations.

You realize that if you go into next week's meeting and recommend that the company pursue the product, he will not be pleased.

He needs the chance to share his view to help the group make the best possible decision. You respect his expertise and believe he can help the team determine the right way to go. You also don't want him feeling ambushed by you. You see that you need to speak with him before the meeting, and let him know that you want him to share his perspectives and his evidence. You are grateful that the model made you aware of this.

BEING TRUE TO THE WORK

Being True to the Work means helping your company make the right decision about whether to sell this product or not. That seems straightforward. The challenge is that the right decision is far from clear. As the sentiment goes, "It's tough to make predictions, especially about the future."[15] In this case, a strong argument can be made for taking the chance and investing in this product. But, a strong argument can also be made for doing just the opposite.

That makes this a perfect opportunity to bring together a group of bright people who can turn their individual expertise into a communal brain. In this case, Being True to the Work means having the team collaborate to make a better decision. You can set the stage for a great conversation by using some activities that help you compare these two options. You realize you also want to gather additional data to bring to that discussion—data about what it will cost to offer this new product and what changes it might require in the way your company operates.

BEING TRUE TO THE COMPANY

Being True to the Company means stepping back to examine this product in light of overall company direction. Is there anything in company goals that encourages or discourages going ahead? For instance, is the company interested in making pet collar sales a bigger portion of its total business? That would encourage offering this product. What other changes in direction is the company contemplating (or is the market demanding) that need to be factored into this decision)?

You are pretty sure that company executives are seriously considering these questions. But to be certain, you add an item to your meeting agenda to discuss this project in relation to overall company directions. This model has again contributed to the richness of your discussion.

HOW THE MARKET DIRECTOR BRINGS THE INDIVIDUAL SKILLS TOGETHER

Now that you have assessed this pet collar product decision from each the four perspectives sequentially, it's time to come to some conclusions. The second, third, and fourth skills were fairly straightforward and offered important ideas that you might have overlooked. Having integrated what you learned from these three areas, you now know it's time to make a decision about the first skill: Being True to Yourself.

The model is now stretched out of balance. Because the other three were quickly resolved, you are spending proportionately more time on that first skill, Being True to Yourself.

This is not necessarily a bad thing. When we are having a hard time figuring out our thoughts on one of these four skills, the perspectives we gain from the other three might lend some perspective. We can ask ourselves, "In this situation what would it look like to be True to Myself while also Being True to Others, True to the Work, and True to the Company?"

When you originally explored what it meant to be true to yourself, you thought it meant either: countering the results of your market research and recommending that your company sell pet collars using this inventor's innovation, or going with the results of your research (even though you didn't agree with it) to preserve the credibility of your research in the future.

Here's what it looks like visually, when the Being True Model is stretched out of balance because one of the four perspectives is more vague or stands out for some other reason.

The 'Being True' Model:
Out of Balance

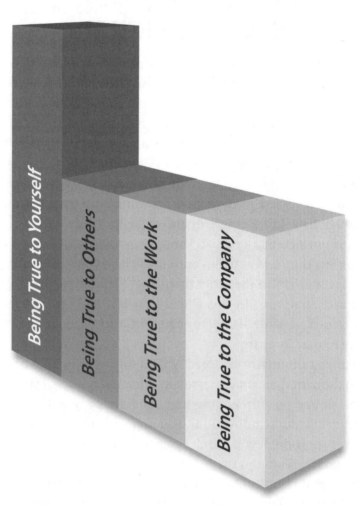

Graphic by Eileen Zornow

When you think about what Being True to Yourself means now, you realize that it isn't an either/or choice. You realize that Being True to Yourself means sharing your research findings and also sharing your intuitive feelings that this pet collar is a good product for your company. Then you engage the team in exploring both those options with the help of your engineering peer, others in the room, and data about the work and the company. Then together as a group, you can come to the right decision.

You arrive at this new conclusion because you trust the team to hear your points in context. You do not have to worry about the future of market research. You know that your colleagues value market data and the views you represent. Because of that trust, you know you can openly share the two opposing perspectives. You feel equipped to facilitate that conversation because of the coordinated forethought supplied by using this model.

APPLYING THE FOUR INDIVIDUAL SKILLS TO A REAL WORK CHALLENGE

Now you have a chance to try the four individual skills for yourself.

 APPLICATION

Think of an important work-related challenge that involves working with others. When you think of Being True to Yourself in relation to this challenge, what occurs to you? Do your values influence you in any way regarding this issue or how it's being handled? Do you have any personal goals regarding this issue? What are you feeling about this issue? How do you need to manage your emotions when it comes to this challenge?

Next, consider what Being True to Others means here? Who else needs to be involved in this issue? How do you need to involve them? Do you already have a connection with those people or do you need to build it?

Your next consideration is what it means to be True to the Work. How can you help leverage that communal brain to arrive at the best thinking regarding this issue? What different views do people have that you know about at this point? How can you explore those and other differences with an open mind, so that the best ideas will prevail?

Finally, how can you be True to the Company? What bigger issues or goals should influence this issue? What does your company most need regarding this challenge? How can you add these company-wide considerations to your conversations on this issue?

Now, take a moment to think about how the process worked, using these four skills. Did considering your challenge from each of these four perspectives enhance your thinking? Do you see things any differently now? Did it lead you to any additional conclusions or actions? Were you able to apply all four skills? Or did you lack skills in some of these areas?

Chapter 6 will give you tips regarding the first two skills, Being True to Yourself and to Others. Chapter 7 offers methods for increasing your skills related to Being True to the Work and the Company.

6

THE FIRST TWO INDIVIDUAL SKILLS: BEING TRUE TO YOURSELF AND TRUE TO OTHERS

Being True to Yourself means understanding your values, goals, and emotions. But that's just the starting point. Beyond being aware of your values, it means living in accord with them. Beyond having goals, it means figuring out how to achieve them. Beyond merely being aware of your emotions, it means managing them.

The following tips are for clarifying your values and goals, and managing your emotions.

GETTING IN TOUCH WITH YOUR VALUES

Step 1: Who are the people you most admire? They might be alive or dead, or people you know personally or through your reading. What do you admire about them? What values do they live by? Which of their values do you most relate to? Take a moment to list those values.

Next, ask yourself: What's important to me in life? What words describe the values by which I live, or would like to? Add those words to your list.

Examples of values that might be important to you include: authenticity, achievement, autonomy, balance, career, caring, collaboration, connection, creativity, equality, family, fitness, generosity, hard work, health, helping others, honesty, integrity, learning, leadership, punctuality, prosperity, reliability, religion, spirituality, strength, success, tradition, wisdom.

Step 2: You should now have a profile of the values that matter to you. If there are more than 10, narrow them down. Why is each one important? Use those reasons to shorten the list.

Step 3: Now prioritize your list of values. Which one is most important to you? Which comes next? This prioritization process is important because there are times when some values may conflict with each other. When that happens, you need to know which is most important.

For example, two of your values might be family and career success. Both of these values could involve significant investments of time. Because time is limited for most of us, there may be times when you need to choose one over the other. How will you do that? If you thought this conflict of values through ahead of time, you might be more likely to select the value that leaves you feeling most contented.

Step 4: Once you have your prioritized list, keep it handy. Use it as a reminder to think about your values and whether you are living in harmony with them. You might even task yourself with thinking about your values every day (for instance, while you are commuting to or from work).[1]

SETTING YOUR GOALS

There are many reasons to set goals. One of the best, in my opinion, is that having goals is empowering. My work with both leaders and employees verifies what Brian Tracy and other experts have found: Achieving goals is one of the best ways to build your self-esteem.

Goals also help you prioritize the things that are most important to you over momentary pleasures. This is particularly important at work. Reminding yourself of your bigger goals can help you avoid doing things that are harmful. For instance, if you remember that your bigger goal is becoming a leader, it may help you find a more appropriate way of expressing your feelings than yelling at someone when you're upset.

SMART is a well-known acronym designed to help people create effective goals. By considering all of these five areas, you can craft goals that are more useful to you.

- ◗ **"S" stands for** *specific.* Articulate your goal in enough detail. Ask yourself why and where is this goal relevant? Include that in the wording of your goal.
- ◗ **"M" represents** *measurable.* Include an element in your goal that enables you to determine your progress toward it and know when you have reached it.
- ◗ **"A" denotes** *attainable.* Set goals that are a stretch but not beyond your ability. If you create impossible goals, you may be tempted to give up. If too many of your goals are easily achievable then you may find the goal-setting process of little value.
- ◗ **"R" signifies** *realistic.* A goal is realistic if you are both willing and able to pursue it. You either have the skills to achieve the goal now or know that you can build the knowledge you need.
- ◗ **"T" means** *timely.* When do you want to accomplish this goal? Insert a date that will give you incentive to achieve that goal within a time period that's relevant to you.

The following tips can help you finalize and achieve your goals once you've created them.

○ Do you have hidden goals related to any of your stated goals? If you have a hidden goal that you also want to achieve in addition to the voiced one, then create an additional goal. If your hidden goal is the real one, then replace your original one. If your hidden goal is not in your best interest, let go of it. For instance, imagine that you set a goal to earn your MBA by June 2020, but your real goal is to attain the position of vice president in your company. Because all of the current VPs have MBAs you made the assumption that getting one is a prerequisite for being considered for a VP position. Have you talked with company leadership to verify that? If not, you may have set the wrong goal when it comes to achieving your real goal of becoming a VP.

○ State your goal in positive terms. Focus on what you want to achieve rather than what you want to move away from. Positive goals that move us toward something we want are more inspiring than negative goals.

○ Visualize yourself achieving this goal. Remind yourself of how it will feel when you are successful.

○ Determine what you need to do to achieve the goal. Create an action plan. What steps will you take and when? Who else might you need to involve? Include those actions on your daily calendar. Consider these commitments every bit as important as others that you make.

USING EMOTIONS TO YOUR ADVANTAGE

In the wise words of Ambrose Bierce, "Speak when you are angry and you will make the best speech you will ever regret."[2]

Being able to use our e-motional energy appropriately starts with being aware of our emotions as they happen. Recognizing that we have emotions coursing through us is a crucial first step. Once we realize we are having an emotional reaction, the next step is to figure out what we are feeling and why.

IDENTIFYING YOUR EMOTIONS

Research shows that only a third of us can identify our emotions as they are happening. The rest of us can't. [3] If we are unaware of what we are experiencing then we can't manage it. The good news is that we can learn. We can build our emotional intelligence and use our emotions to benefit us. What follows is a practical approach for identifying and understanding your emotions as they occur. (This process emphasizes negative emotions because most of us don't need assistance in recognizing or dealing with positive emotions.)

1. **Recognize that you are feeling negatively about something.** Notice that you are having a reaction, that you have e-motional energy coursing through you. This means that you need to become aware of what is happening.

2. **Identify your feelings.** Ask yourself what you are experiencing. Are you having a physical reaction? Are your shoulder muscles tight? Do you have a knot in your stomach? Now figure out what you are feeling. Are you confused, angry, disappointed, or hurt? It might take some time before you are proficient at naming your feelings quickly and accurately. Stick with it. It gets easier with practice.

3. **Take a moment to explore what you're feeling.** It's best if you can find a quiet spot to focus inward for a few moments. That is often hard to do while you are interacting with others. It is much easier if you can take a brief time-out to figure out what is going on, and decide what you want to do about it.

   — If you are alone, then taking this time-out is easy. It's still relatively easy when you are with people that you are comfortable enough with to excuse yourself briefly. If you are in a work situation, you can often remove yourself briefly with a trip to the rest room.

   — If you cannot remove yourself physically, you might be able to focus inward for a moment while staying

physically present. William Ury[4] dubbed this as
"going to the balcony" (taking a step back and analyzing what is happening as if you were not involved
in it).

— If it isn't possible for you to step back and focus
inward in the moment, then pause and explore your
emotions as soon as you can.

4. **Calm down.** When trying to understand what we're feeling, the tendency is to throw ourselves further into those
feelings. However, when we are still deeply engrossed in
them, it's difficult to gain perspective and examine our
feelings neutrally. They tend to control us rather than us
managing them. Once your emotions are no longer in
control of you, you can manage them. So take a brief
break from your reaction. Think about something positive until you feel yourself calming down. For some
it's thinking about a loved one, for others it may be a
beloved pet.

Now that you are aware of your emotions, the next step is gain-
ing control over them.

MANAGING YOUR EMOTIONS

The inability to manage our emotions can hurt us, especially when
we're dealing with other people. The way we behave when we're not
in control can lead others to stop trusting us and can blind us to seeing their ideas. I was impressed to hear what one of the Silicon Valley
leaders had to say on this topic: "There's always an external excuse
for why things happen to me. We are removing those excuses and
looking at ourselves as empowered people who can and do impact
what happens around us."

Self-management means we are aware of our reactions and can
handle our emotional responses. It means being thoughtful about
whether or not to express our feelings to others, and how to do it
appropriately if we decide to share them. It also means figuring out

how to release those emotions in a useful way if it is not appropriate to express them directly.

A lot of us are more comfortable exploring what we think than what we feel. If you are one of those people, this is a great time to realize that exploring your feelings as carefully as you do your thoughts can provide you great benefits.

The following four steps offer a process for how to manage your emotions.

1. **Determine the spark that triggered your reaction.** What caused it? What was said or done? How was it said? What about it bothered you? Was it the content? Or the tone of voice?

2. **Expand your interpretation.** Think about that incident that sparked your reaction. If it was the person's tone of voice, what did you infer from it? If it was the content of what was said, what assumptions did you make that caused your reaction?

   — Realize that your initial interpretation might be incorrect. Allow yourself to explore other ones. It means putting your first explanation aside for a time. You can return to it later if it turns out that it was accurate.

   — Ask yourself what else might explain what was said or done. Try to come up with several possible explanations. Try assuming positive intent on the part of the other person or people involved. Does that change how you interpret their words and actions?

   — Do your alternate interpretations change your feelings? Do these new interpretations give you empathy for others who were involved? Do they help you see that others may not have meant for their action to affect you the way it did?

   — Ask yourself: Am I so focused on what's going on in the moment that I am losing track of more important goals?

— If you feel your first interpretation was right, you still have a choice when it comes to how you will act. You may discover other genuine feelings that help you "Be True to Yourself" while also maintaining an effective work relationship with that person. For instance, after looking for other interpretations you still feel Susan was wrong to accuse you of not doing enough research. In thinking about the cause of her statement, you realize that she was frustrated with you and others because she had been trying to join the conversation for a while and hadn't been able to jump in. Her behavior was inappropriate, as she wasn't managing her emotions well. Seeing the reasons behind it allows you to excuse her.

3. **Take actions.** What actions can you take to diffuse your e-motional energy effectively?

— Based on what you just went through do you need to take any actions to resolve this issue? What are they?

— Do you have any lingering e-motional energy that you cannot express and still need to diffuse in a healthy way? Getting physical exercise is a great way to release energy (for instance, taking a walk during your lunch hour). You can also ask friends or coworkers to engage in peer coaching. Agree that you will offer "safe-zones" to each other to help process things that happen. Contact one of them to give you additional perspectives or to help you redirect any remaining energy in a productive way.

4. **Pause to congratulate yourself.** You've done a great job of self-coaching. You've used your reactions to help you be more effective, rather than leaving them to bubble up inappropriately.

By engaging in this process consistently, you not only resolve the current issue, you also raise your EQ. It forms new "grooves" in your brain that lead you to behave in these new ways moving forward.

THE TAKE AWAY

Being aware of your values and your goals, and acting in accord with them as much as you can, will bring you contentment both in work and in your personal life. The same is true for increasing awareness of your emotions and your ability to manage them. Being True to Yourself in these ways will help you work better with others.

The tools involved in this first skill of Being True to Yourself are for you to apply personally (compared to some of the other skills in which team or company practices play an important role). That said, it's easier to have a commitment to develop ourselves if the company culture fosters it. You can assist your company in fostering a culture that helps employees Be True to Themselves. Talk to your manager and tell him or her what a difference it makes when management encourages such growth.

One Silicon Valley leader told me this about her workplace: "I've worked for this company for many years. Every step of the way, from one group to another, there has always been space for me to learn to be better. Not because people thought I was deficient, but to grow personally and professionally. This company encourages and allows us to stretch and learn and grow."

 APPLICATION

Can you use these tips to help you clarify your values? Do you have goals for yourself and strategies for achieving them? Were you able to refine your goals with the skills provided? How would you assess yourself when it comes to harnessing your emotions? Why don't you try using this process now to get better control of something that you are currently feeling?

TIPS FOR BEING TRUE TO OTHERS

In some workplaces, reaching out to help others seems foreign. People cannot conceive of how or why they would do this. In contrast, in the workplace cultures I studied while formulating the Silicon Valley Approach to Collaboration, people can't conceive of not supporting others.

When we understand the value of connecting with others we act differently. One of the Silicon Valley leaders I spoke with stressed that "we need a safe environment where people feel free to express their opinions. We need to be able to ask any question. And we need to feel we are all accountable. That we own the results together."

In this kind of culture, blamestorming is replaced with brainstorming.

Another Silicon Valley leader put it this way: "If you are competitive, hoarding, and not helping others, your coworkers see you as selfish. Most of these people eventually select out and choose to leave our company." That's one of the aspects of Silicon Valley firms' cultures. They encourage trust, respect, and sharing so strongly that people who don't share these values usually feel that there is a mismatch and leave.

HOW TO CONNECT WITH OTHERS

Some simple behaviors can help you be more conscious of others and create connections with them. They include:

- **Consciously build bonds.** The weaker the connection we have with others, the harder it is to work effectively with them. When we build respectful relationships, it strengthens our ability to work together. It isn't hard to do.

  — Reach out and get to know your coworkers. Don't wait for them to show interest in you and your ideas first.
  — Involve folks, ask them their views, and listen with genuine interest.

— Offer suggestions for alternatives rather than just complaining.

— Seek ways to help colleagues. Don't always expect something in return.

O **Prepare ourselves to listen as consciously as we prepare to speak.** Most of us see the value in organizing our thoughts before we speak. It helps us be more logical. Very few of us take the time to prepare ourselves to listen. It is just as important and results in a positive difference when we do.

O **Listen for possibilities.** Some of us believe we add the most value by criticizing what others have just said. We listening reactively with the intent of finding the flaws. Instead, what if you decided to listen proactively for the possibilities? Many conversations would be quite different.

O **Speak in ways that encourage others to listen.** Phrase things in ways that intrigue others and engage their curiosity rather than putting them on the defense. Saying, "Your idea won't work because of X," is likely to shut down the conversation or encourage the other person to argue. Instead, you might say, "You have a point with your idea to move in Y direction. If 'X' were to happen, how would we deal with that?"

O **Remember that emotions play a part in every discussion.** If we become more aware of our own and other people's feelings, we start seeing what is going on beneath the surface. If we ignore those feelings, they may seep out in unproductive ways.

O **Seek value from every relationship, especially the challenging ones.**

Commenting on the commitment employees make to connect with others, one Silicon Valley leader mused: "Employees working together is like going to church every day even though you are not a saint. Democracy isn't about [only] voting every two or four years.

Individuals here have that kind of commitment to the team and the company. We're willing to work with others on an ongoing basis, even when it's hard."

INQUIRY BEFORE ADVOCACY

The connections that we work hard to create with coworkers can be strengthened or weakened depending on how we act when we are working together. If we value the views of others, then we need to show it.

Two tools that most of us use in group interactions are inquiry and advocacy. We use inquiry for exploring topics and gathering information. We advocate for certain ideas over others when we are ready to narrow our thinking and make decisions. Both of these tools can enhance connections between coworkers or hurt those connections. How we use these skills determines whether we strengthen or weaken the connections that we worked hard to create.

Say you are a member of a new project team. The agenda for today's meeting is to talk about what's needed going forward. Based on your previous experience, you believe the team needs senior management support, more resources, and clearer expectations. The facilitator introduces the topic of the meeting and asks people to share their thoughts.

You have a choice to make: You could jump in and advocate for these three items, doing your best to convince others that there's no need to brainstorm further, or you could give others a chance to speak first and see what emerges.

We often prematurely jump to advocating our views, but doing that can defeat the goal of having an open dialogue to fill gaps in knowledge. Others may have worthy ideas regarding project needs in addition to your three. If you jump to advocacy, those other ideas may not emerge. Generally, inquiry is most effective when it precedes advocacy. This gives good ideas a chance to come to light before participants narrow their perspective and advocate for certain solutions. With the understanding that inquiry should come first, let's focus on the best ways to use this tool.

EFFECTIVE INQUIRY

⊙ Introduce the topic with enough detail. Ensure that attendees are clear about the goals and the scope of the discussion. What will success look like? What are the criteria that will tell you when you have succeeded? One of the goals of inquiry is to expand the group's knowledge about the topic.

⊙ Encourage participants who have something to contribute to share their views. Take time to understand and explore the perspectives that seem to hold the most promise.

⊙ Establish a norm of sharing reasons and assumptions behind points of view, and assessing whether they hold true for this situation.

⊙ Ask questions that encourage participants to think more deeply and share new ideas. A variety of activities can help you do this. For instance, you can construct an analogy to turn the conversation in a certain direction or brainstorm similarities between seemingly disparate objects to help attendees see connections between several work topics.

⊙ Clarify what has been said to avoid misunderstandings or differing interpretations.

⊙ Before you close the conversation, ensure that participants have what they need and are ready to move to next steps.

Once you are certain that you have accomplished your goals for the inquiry, you can now move to the next step, which is often narrowing your options to the best ones.

SUCCESSFUL ADVOCACY

⊙ Set the parameters of this portion of the meeting, outlining the goals and how the group will know when they have been reached. One of the goals of advocacy is usually to narrow options down to an appropriate number.

- Next, attendees should compare the options, telling the group which idea they believe is best and why. They should back their opinions with evidence, and disclose any assumptions they have made. (A process that you can use to compare options will be offered in Chapter 7.) It's particularly helpful if the speaker can reveal new thinking or insights that were not entirely obvious to the group.

- The group should actively seek disconfirming evidence for the options that are rising as the most feasible. Look for conflicting information that may reveal weaknesses of which you were previously unaware. If you can't find any it may mean that you have done a thorough job in your considerations, or it may mean you haven't dug deep enough. Wouldn't you rather find and consider those factors now than let them cause your project to fail?

- Remember that the goal is not only to reach the best idea for this project but also for the company.

- It's crucial to remember that the advocacy process doesn't give you license to simply push your view and expect others to agree. You need to convince others with facts. Present the logic and assumptions you are making and let the discussion take its course. If your position is strong enough it should prevail.

APPLICATION

Most of us are more comfortable with either inquiry or with advocacy. How well do you use each of these two sets of skills? Do you
rate yourself strongly in using inquiry skills? How successfully do
you use advocacy? After you've done a self-assessment, ask others
for feedback. Do they confirm how you see yourself or do they see
you differently? Remember that your objective is to increase your
abilities to objectively use both inquiry and advocacy.

$$\boxed{7}$$

THE OTHER INDIVIDUAL SKILLS: BEING TRUE TO THE WORK AND TRUE TO THE COMPANY

The vast majority of us see ourselves as being True to the Work. But doing that when we are working alone is quite different than when we are working with others. It's more of a challenge to Be True to the Work when working in a team because we often have such different perspectives. The teams that get labelled as "special" are the ones that merge disparate views well. Two of the key proficiencies that help a team achieve this synergy are Being Open to New Information and Exploring the Options.

OUR OPENNESS TO NEW INFORMATION

There is usually far more information available to us than what we take in. Our brain lets in only a portion of the available stimuli.

Some of this takes place at a sub-conscious level. Some of it happens consciously when we knowingly make decisions about what to take in and what to ignore.

We can improve our ability to let in more of the relevant information and filter out things that are less relevant. We can train our brain to do a better job of situational analysis (quickly assessing our environment, figuring out what's going on, and making sense of it). As a result, we will be "seeing beyond images; hearing beyond words; and sensing beyond appearances."[1]

Four tools are particularly useful for training our brain to gather and use information more effectively: Noticing What We Are Seeing, Scanning for Relevant Details, Using Our Senses to Gather Information, and Seeing the Patterns in Information. (Alex Bennet, former Chief Knowledge Officer for the U.S. Department of Navy, was instrumental in developing these tools.[2]) When folks on a team use these four skills, the team will function at a higher level. What follows are some exercises that can expand our skills in these four areas.

NOTICING WHAT WE ARE SEEING

Most of us multitask more often than we realize. When we sit in a room or walk between buildings, we are deep in thought. At times we may focus on our surrounding environment. More often, though, we don't. We may be thinking about the meeting we're about to attend or something our manager just said. Or even that we need to pick up milk at the grocery store on the way home from work. We aren't actively noticing what's around us. We're on automatic pilot, letting our brain decide subconsciously what to let in.

By consciously observing more, we can train our brain to do a better job of noticing what is important. This doesn't mean that we stop multitasking forever. That's not something that most people want to do. Rather, we are taking brief breaks from it to teach our brain to do better at filtering on its own.

One way to stretch our capacity to notice more is to practice repetitive observation and recall. Think about a room that you visit regularly (one that you are not in at the moment). Write down every detail you can remember about this room and its contents. Then visit the room and compare your memory to what actually exists. Add items that you missed to your list.

A few days later, repeat this exercise. Without looking at your revised list, recall as much as you can about that room and again write it down. Then return to the room and see if you did any better. Did you remember or forget things that you added from your first return visit? What else did you see on this newest visit that you hadn't noticed on your first return?

Continue to practice this exercise with different locations. It should begin to improve the amount that you notice and can later recall. And it will translate to enhanced noticing in other aspects of your life. For instance, your team should be able to design a much better game if you notice how a variety of customers do in playing the game and notice what's going on when they're having difficulties performing certain commands.

SCANNING FOR RELEVANT DETAILS

Scanning is the act of taking large amounts of data and narrowing them down to the details most relevant for a particular situation. As we train ourselves to notice even more of the information in our environment, we need a better way to retain what is useful and filter out the rest. Scanning is like "speed reading our environment."[3]

Practice the art of scanning the next time you are in a room that is new to you. Take a moment to quickly look around and then make a mental snapshot of what you are seeing. Count the number of tables and chairs and how they are positioned. Note colors and textures. Next, close your eyes and mentally document those things. Don't capture any of this in writing, because this activity is about remembering. As you leave the room, take another quick look around to reinforce the details you scanned earlier. A few days later, when you are in a different physical setting, take a few moments to recall important descriptors of that room. A few months later, see if you can still remember most of those descriptors.

The idea isn't to go back and double-check and increase the number of details you remember, as you did in the noticing exercise. Here, the goal is to improve your ability to scan an environment quickly, commit relevant descriptors to memory, and be able to recall them later when you need them.

Conduct this exercise regularly when you are in new settings. Over time, you will see an improvement in your ability to scan and determine what to capture in your memory. If members of your team work on improving this skill, your collective abilities will likewise improve.

USING OUR SENSES

Sensing means using as many of our five senses as possible when we gather information. Of course, we have physiological limits. Some of us have permanent visual or hearing impairments. Many of us have a temporarily reduced sense of smell when we have a cold. Putting those limitations aside, it's safe to say that most of us could make better use of our five senses to take in information.

Increasing our use of sight means more than just seeing things in greater detail; it also means seeing things in relationship to other things. This skill helps us to sort and make sense of data we are taking in.

One way to improve your ability to see things in relation to other things is to look at your surroundings from a positional viewpoint. For instance, when you are looking at the sun, notice both its position in the sky and in relation to the horizon. Now, note the time of day. Store that information in your mind. When you see the sun at that position during a certain time of year, you will be able to approximate the time without looking at your watch.

Notice the buildings and other permanent fixtures at a street corner without looking at the street signs. Commit these fixtures to memory and you will be able to recognize this corner without the aid of the street signs in the future.

Increasing your relational abilities can help you and coworkers with a variety of issues at work. Imagine that you are redesigning a hammer that your company sells. In watching a variety of customers use the existing hammer you suddenly notice that the size of the customer's hand and length of fingers affects the ability to use the tool well. When you share this insight with your design team you realize that it might make sense to design hammers with a variety of handle lengths and widths to meet the needs of people with different hand sizes. You embark on more research in this area and arrive at an entirely new set of offerings for your company. Chances are that you wouldn't have noticed this until you improved your ability to see things relationally.

Our hearing also helps us to comprehend what is going on around us. Auditory clues provide all sorts of information that augment the data that we take in visually. Try this exercise: Close your eyes and focus on what you're hearing. What conversations are going on? Do you hear people walking? Other sounds?

Once you have identified those sounds determine where they are in relation to you without looking. Where are the talking people located? In which direction do you hear footsteps? Are they coming toward you or moving away? Once you are adept at identifying sounds close to you, train yourself to hear more faint sounds.

The following is an additional sensory exercise: The next time you are talking with someone, focus on their non-verbal clues. What does his facial expression imply? Is he sighing or pausing between words? Is he gesturing? What do you think these things mean? Search beyond his words to identify the other signals he is sharing. Only a small portion of what people communicate is through words. The more skilled you become at reading those non-verbal signals the better you will understand other people's thoughts and feelings.

SEEING THE PATTERNS

Seeing patterns is a vital skill in an environment packed with information. As we expand our ability to notice, to scan, and to take in sensory data, we need a way to quickly analyze all that information. This skill is about noticing patterns. When you are in a group, practice seeing patterns in what people wear. How many are wearing dark colors or short-sleeved shirts? Are there logos on the shirts?

Begin to notice patterns between different rooms in a building or different restaurants.

The next time you are standing in line, instead of focusing on your mobile device, look around and see if you can detect any patterns in what you are seeing. Over time, you should notice an improvement in your ability to see patterns in all sorts of data, including employee or customer satisfaction surveys, problems related to a product you are creating, and other aspects of your work world. Imagine your team using heightened patterning abilities. The teams that do the best are the ones that are made up of people with strong patterning abilities.

 APPLICATION

The exercises to improve your noticing, scanning, sensing, and patterning skills can be fun. They're especially enjoyable when you start noticing *improvements* in your skills. Why don't you try the first one—Noticing—for two weeks? Then try the exercises related to Scanning for the next two weeks. Next, move to Using Your Senses for two weeks. Finally, spend two weeks increasing your Patterning skills. Even better, consider getting your team to commit to improving these skills together. You will see a positive improvement in the quality of your work.

Now let's move on to two tools that can assist your team in analyzing options more effectively.

EXPLORING THE OPTIONS

When we engage in a lively discussion about options we are analyzing, sometimes things move smoothly to common understandings and decisions. The right ideas emerge quickly. The group easily achieves consensus. At other times, that isn't the case and getting to joint conclusions is more challenging.

We often assume that speed to consensus is desirable. We all have other tasks waiting for us. Additionally, lack of clarity can be uncomfortable. Disagreements can become heated. These unpleasant feelings can encourage us to just plow forward, but sometimes that's not the best thing to do.

I can offer you a simple process for analyzing and comparing ideas and options in situations when you want to reach consensus and move ahead with one of them, but you're having a hard time.

SYSTEMATIC BELIEF AND DOUBT

When we support an idea, we notice aspects of it that are better than other ideas, and see the ways it can help us move toward our goals. (Let's call this "engaging in a Belief Search.") When we do not support an idea, we tend to look for aspects of that idea that are weak and could mean failure. (Let's call this a "Doubt Search.") Using a structured Belief/Doubt approach, we can all engage in both sides together rather than some of us gathering evidence to prove the strength of the idea while others look for evidence that shows its inherent weakness. Doing so helps the group do a better job of evaluating options and making the best choice.

Peter Elbow[4] originated the idea and, in working with companies over the years, I have evolved it into this activity. It consists of just two steps. First, the whole group engages in the Belief Search. Everyone looks for the parts of the idea that are true and that make it workable. Only after they have done that thoroughly does the whole group move on to engage in a Doubt Search, seeking to uncover the parts of the idea that work against its succeeding.

While engaged in the Belief Search, the group needs to agree not to move on to the Doubt step until everyone can see the significant parts of the idea that are persuasive. The work of this step is to find those areas of strength. First, everyone in the group needs to understand the idea. What evidence supports it? What are its intriguing features? When might this idea be true and useful? The questions we ask should help identify positive aspects of the idea. Those of us who believe in the idea should help others see it from our point of view. And we need to share the evidence and interpretations that led us to those positive interpretations.

Those of us who are skeptical should agree to explore those strengths until we can understand them. That means being willing to listen with an open mind. Team members may not reject the idea until they have succeeded in believing in it. One of the secrets of believing is that we have to invest ourselves in the idea and in liking it. We are not just going along to go along. If we are finding it difficult to agree, we need to keep working at it until we genuinely see the positive points that others see.

Once the group has a full view of the strengths associated with the idea, we move on to the Doubt Search. Now it's time to critique the idea and explore its flaws. During this step, participants shouldn't remain so attached to the idea's strengths that we are unable to see its frailties. Look for aspects of the idea that might make it unworkable. Look for inconsistencies that may have gone unnoticed during the Belief Search. Explore the circumstances under which this idea might be unworkable.

With all participating fully in both the Belief and the Doubt Searches, the discussion becomes a dialogue in which everyone works together to discover the best courses of action. Participants usually discover an idea's strengths that they weren't previously seeing, and also uncover weaknesses they hadn't been aware of. This gives them a more complete picture from which to make the decision. And they listen to each other and both the pros and cons related to the options much better than traditional discussions in which everyone is advocating for their own choices.

Because this process does take time and energy it should be reserved for tasks that are important, and for the options that have the most potential, rather than all the options that have arisen from a brainstorming session. This Belief/Doubt Search can be particularly useful in cases when you don't have enough hard facts at the beginning of the discussion to form a sound conclusion.

One leader I interviewed shared a striking difference between the firm where he currently works and another company in the same industry where he used to work. At his previous workplace, employees believed they were more knowledgeable and capable of great conclusions than others. That view led them to have a higher regard for their own ideas and lower regard for ideas shared by others. This resulted in very little real consideration of ideas shared by others. He struggled to express how suffocating the workplace had been. It undermined the company's success because employees rarely used their communal brain to examine ideas together. He left and found a company with a very different culture. He is convinced that this openness to ideas of others is crucial to effective collaboration. So am I.

The Belief/Doubt process helps us create that collaborative company culture. It also reduces group-think, a phenomenon in which team members begin to think too much alike and become so supportive of others that we don't challenge each other to come to great solutions.

WHEN WE NEED SOMETHING MORE: INFORMED REVISIONING

At some point in exploring our options, we may find that none of them fully achieves our objectives. We aren't thrilled with any of the possibilities. We suspect that continuing the current dialogue in the same direction isn't likely to lead to a magical solution. However, we are fairly certain that we've come up with the most feasible options. This means that starting over isn't likely to yield better alternatives.

In cases like this, it can help to return to our options and look at them with a new eye. The intent is not to create an entirely new slate of options, but to scrutinize the ones already on the table in a different way, informed by the analysis we already conducted, along with some new thoughts. The ideal is to use this new thinking to arrive at a new option that combines some of the best parts of the existing ideas.

In order to do this, we need to identify and examine the advantages (or upsides) and disadvantages (or downsides) of our options.

The following image represents a worksheet you can use to capture the brainstorming and assist you in finding that new option.

First, list each of the options under consideration. Then identify the upsides and downsides of each of those options. Find the most important pluses and minuses of each option.

Now it's time to get creative and craft a new solution. This solution will integrate as many of the salient upsides from all of those existing options as possible, while minimizing as many significant downsides as you can. You are creating a new option, but not one from scratch. Rather, that new option will re-organize and re-combine important aspects of your previous ideas into new thinking and a new possibility.

It is important to keep in mind that your new solution is not meant to be a compromise between these various options, but instead an inspired integration of aspects that work together to meet your needs.

Informed Revisioning Worksheet

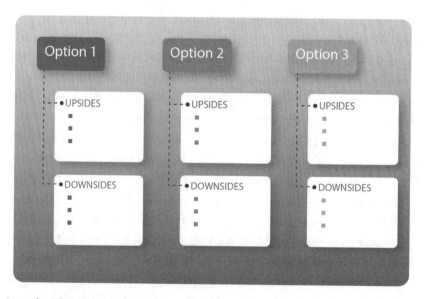

Image by Eileen Zornow

It might help to see an example of Informed Revisioning. Let's say you are a leader at a Mexican-fusion fast-food chain. The executives of the chain have decided to expand the number of restaurants. You and three other leaders have the job of determining what type of expansion would be most likely to contribute to the overall success of your company.

After much research, your team has come up with the following three options: expand by increasing the number of your branded, Mexican-fusion restaurants in several already-successful markets; expand by moving into some new geographies and establishing a presence for your chain in those new markets; expand by opening some fast-food burger restaurants in several of your already-successful markets.

You have spent weeks working together on this important project. The whiteboards in your meeting room are full of facts and figures. Piles of paper hold copies of PowerPoint presentations, spreadsheets crammed with data, and images. You have conducted exhaustive research.

The four of you have examined the options in detail and you are surprised that despite all of the work you've put into it, none of the options rise above the other two as the best. You have even talked about whether you should start over and try to discover another option—one that might stand out more favorably than any of these three. After consideration, however, you agree that going back to the starting place doesn't seem like it will yield any better or different solutions. You decide to use Informed Revisioning. This is what you come up with:

STEP 1

Identify the upsides and downsides of your three options. You do that and come up with the following options. (For the sake of this example I have identified only two upsides and downsides for each option. When using Informed Revisioning on a real issue, you will likely identify many more than this.)

Option 1: Expand by increasing the number of Mexican-fusion restaurants in several already successful markets.

Upsides include:

- O You can use existing supply chains and distribution centers to stock the new restaurants, saving money.
- O You can similarly capitalize on existing advertising, saving money in this area as well.

Downsides include:

- O People who like your food might already be visiting your restaurants. The new restaurants may cannibalize a lot of business from your current sites.
- O You may have set up restaurants in the best locations already, and further expansion in your current markets will not be supported with enough new business to be profitable.

Option 2: Expand by moving into some new geographies and establishing a presence for your chain in those new markets.
Upsides include:

- O If some percentage (say, 33 percent) of everyone in the United States likes Mexican-fusion fast food, then you can expand your success by getting 33 percent of a whole new market.
- O Adding new markets enables you to get closer to purchasing national advertising, which is often more cost-efficient than localized advertising.

Downsides include:

- O You can't capitalize on existing supply chain and distribution centers, so these costs will be higher.
- O When you move into new markets you can't leverage existing brand awareness and word-of-mouth.

Option 3: Expand by opening several fast-food burger restaurants in several already-successful markets.

Upsides include:

- Even though these restaurants will serve different menu items, you can still use existing supply chains and distribution centers to stock the new restaurants, saving some money.
- You are not cannibalizing current business because you will presumably tap a different audience with these burger restaurants than you do with your Mexican-fusion restaurants.

Downsides include:

- Although you can use your existing supply chain and distribution centers, you need to stock different foods and accessories, increasing your costs and increasing the complexity of managing your inventory.
- Advertising to establish and maintain two brands in these markets will cost more.

Informed Revisioning Example: Summary of Restaurant Expansion Decision

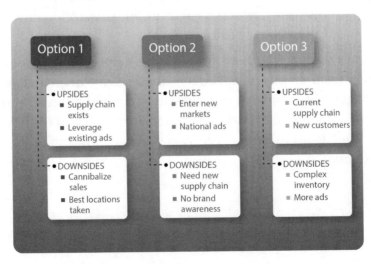

Graphic by Eileen Zornow

STEP 2

Craft a new solution that integrates as many of the salient upsides of the three options as possible while minimizing as many significant downsides as you can.

○ After examining all of these upsides and downsides it becomes clear that the best solution is to have a multi-pronged approach. You decide to recommend to your executives that:

— In several markets where your stores are not any-where near the 33-percent saturation, you decide to add several more Mexican-fusion restaurants.

— In markets where your stores are nearing the 33-percent saturation and where market tests show lack of interest in another burger restau-rant, you decide to move your current brand into adjacent markets to capitalize on some exist-ing advertising, supply chain, and distribution centers.

— In several markets where you are saturating the 33 percent and where market tests indicate inter-est in a new burger restaurant, you decide to test a few burger restaurants.

Engaging in Informed Revisioning helped these leaders see things from a new perspective. This activity helped them see that they didn't have to just choose one of the three options. It allowed them to come to new conclusions and make strong rec-ommendations to their executives that they wouldn't otherwise have thought of.

WHEN TO FISH AND WHEN TO CUT BAIT

When we are dealing with constraints such as time, money, or staff resources, it sometimes makes the most sense to just select the best option at-hand and implement it. This is called "satisficing," a term that was coined in the 1940s by Herbert Simon, a Nobel Prize winner and renowned management expert. Combining the words *satisfy* and *suffice*, it describes those situations when an optimal solution is not likely to be found so we go with the best one that we have.

At other times, however, satisficing isn't the best thing to do. What if Tesla had satisficed when they were trying to build their first all-electric car? If they had stopped before they found the right formula, they might have ended up designing just another very good hybrid rather than the industry-changing car that they built. On the other hand, what if Tesla had spent five more years trying to get the formula right and still had not found the right design? In that case, they might have wished they had satisficed.

George Bernard Shaw once said, "Success comes from taking the path of maximum advantage instead of the path of least resistance."[5] Unfortunately, there is no easy formula for determining if we are on the cusp of that next amazing product. Often it is best to satisfice because it does the job and we suspect that many more months of work will not yield the result we want.

This concept is an important one for groups making critical decisions that influence directions of a project or an entire company. Although there is no easy way to determine when to "fish" and when to "cut bait," these decisions are crucially important. If this situation arises, a group needs to discuss whether to keep going or to satisfice.

APPLICATION

How would you rate your own skills when it comes to noticing, scanning, sensing, and pattern detection? Would you be willing to commit to improving your abilities in these four areas? Is there a way for you to introduce the idea of improving these four abilities with a team you're on?

Does your company have a method like the Systematic Belief/ Doubt to encourage employees to come together and make better decisions about the work? Do you have a current situation where none of the options you've come up with seem ideal? Consider leading your coworkers through this Informed Revisioning process.

TIPS FOR BEING TRUE TO THE COMPANY

THE JOURNEY FROM UNDERSTANDING TO BUY-IN

Being True to the Company starts with a clear understanding of the company's directions and buy-in to those directions. Understanding firm-wide goals and strategies is greatly enhanced when employees have an understanding of the context they are operating within. The more we know about our company's mission, which includes why the leaders are passionate about that mission, and our history of achievements, failures, and lessons, the more we become vested in helping our company succeed.

Company goals become our own goals not just because we know that achieving them pays our salary. We are willing to work harder to help make the company successful when we see and understand that bigger picture and when leaders treat us as true partners.

Let's share what this feels like in real life with an example of from one Silicon Valley company.

We launched a new product this year at our company. We knew it would mean an increase in work, but had no idea how much. When the amount of work dawned on us, we were a bit daunted. We thought about saying we just couldn't do it without some support.

We talked informally to some of our leaders. They helped us realize that the company couldn't afford to give us more resources. The company was strapped. They candidly shared that giving us more would just take vital resources from another group. It could jeopardize the success of this new product and our company. The company really needed the additional revenue.

Once those leaders shared what was going on, things fell into place. We leveraged our current roles as much as we could. We divided up the tasks in ways that made sense. Part of it was based on our expertise and location, but we didn't adhere to those roles rigidly. When we needed fresh perspectives or just needed a helping hand, we reallocated the work.

The key was how easy it turned out to be because people bought in completely. Once the leaders entrusted us with information about the real situation, we didn't have to pull anyone along. Our leaders treated us as respected members of the inner circle. They do that regularly. It sets the tone for successes like this to happen.

LEADERSHIP'S ROLE

When leaders provide employees with enough information about their company and company directions, employees respond positively. It is even better when leaders not only share that information, but also the context and the reasons behind decisions. This gives employees the background they need to make the right decisions about their work. It creates a sense of partnership between them and leaders. This kind of partnership leads to commitment rather than compliance.

Clearly, employees cannot make this happen by themselves. Leaders need to supply the information and context that starts this positive cycle of ownership. But any employee can have a role in helping make it happen by talking with their manager and describing what a big difference this can make.

EMPLOYEE'S ROLE

When leaders are doing their part, they are keeping staff informed and treating them as partners. Strategy and tactics are explained in enough detail to give needed context. Employees' views are sought on topics that directly affect them.

The employees' part, in turn, is to keep company goals and strategies in mind when making significant or even small decisions about their work. Quite often there may be conflicts between what is best for a project and what is optimal for the whole company. Doing one's part means making decisions that support company direction, even when it might change or discontinue the project.

For instance, imagine a fun feature you could add to a product you are designing. Say you work at a toy company that sells a toy car. Several of you come up with the idea of adding remote control to the car.

Employees would enjoy learning enough about this feature to make it work well. Evidence tells you that your customers would love this feature. It sounds good, right? Not if this feature is expensive and takes you in a direction that conflicts with your company's overall strategy. In this instance, doing the right thing means letting go of this feature. You may be giving up a pet project, but ideally your leaders will recognize your sacrifice for the good of the company.

The following questions are designed to help you ensure that any project fits into and contributes to your company's goals. You can use some of these questions before you begin a new project to help evaluate the worth of that project in relation to overall company goals. Other questions can be used during your project work to assist you in making the decisions that most benefit your company. You can use these questions on your own or in a group.

1. What are this company's biggest opportunities right now?

2. What have you learned in the last few years that should affect what you do now and during the next year?

3. How can you help ensure that this company will be thriving three to five years from now?

4. What are the biggest challenges, threats, and constraints facing the company right now? How can you and coworkers assist the company in these areas?

5. How can you help achieve company-wide goals?

6. To which company goal does this project contribute?

7. What needs to happen for this project to contribute to that company goal?

8. Is there executive sponsorship for this project? What do executives expect from it?

9. Regularly ask yourself: What is the bigger picture here? If you make a certain decision what is likely to happen? Will that move you toward that bigger company objective?

10. Who do you need to communicate with or make reports to in order to maximize the project's success?

11. What type of final review should be conducted at the conclusion of this project to leverage lessons for other projects?

APPLICATION

The previous questions are intended to assist you in making the right decisions as you plan and implement your work. Do you and others have sufficient context to answer these questions when you are planning your project and when considering day-to-day decisions in carrying out that project? If not, can you speak with company leaders and let them know how much better you could do if you could answer these questions? Let them know that you want to be even more True to the Company and that receiving this information would allow you to do it.

You may have assumed that there was not much you could do as an individual to strengthen collaboration at your company. I hope the four Individual Skills model and these tools for applying that model have changed that belief. If you practice these skills regularly, they will become second nature and will help you to positively affect collaboration at your company.

Now let's look at ways you can strengthen team efforts.

8

AGILE WORK PROCESS: ANYPLACE, ANYTIME

THE VALUE OF AN ALL-PURPOSE FRAMEWORK THAT CAN BE CUSTOMIZED

In Chapter 4, I unveiled the Silicon Valley Approach to Collaboration and explained the three levels: individual skills, team tools, and company practices. When it comes to the team level, it's helpful to have a process to help organize how multiple employees work together.

Having some sort of "scaffolding" is as crucial for teams working on a project in an organization as it is for construction crews building a skyscraper. Although the specifics will vary from project to project, in general team members need a shared understanding of:

- Overall project goals and how they contribute to company-wide objectives.
- How the elements of the project need to be combined to achieve overall goals.
- Who will be involved and what they will do.

- Methods for capturing and sharing important information.
- Types of meetings and communications that will occur.
- Metrics for measuring success.

Mike Kavis summed it up well in his blog: "I would typically scoff at project charters, team structure . . . [etc.]. But [when a] project consists of . . . multiple teams on various systems . . . there has to be some order to the chaos."[1]

The concept of "process" has become a dirty word in some organizations. As one Process Improvement professional recently blogged: "I'll bet many of you, upon reading 'I hate process!' feel just a little better inside, relieved and thinking 'yes, someone finally said it!'."[2]

Why does this simple concept have such a bad reputation? One leader I interviewed explained that the staff in his company believe that as companies grow, so does chaos. In order to stop the chaos, companies tend to develop processes and procedures. But when companies need employees to invent new ways of doing things, they find that staff following rigid processes have lost the ability to be creative and figure out how to do things differently.

How do they deal with this dilemma at his company? They differentiate between good and bad processes. Bad processes create rules for the sake of efficiency rather than effectiveness. They impose rigid bureaucratic requirements that seem to have very little purpose. Good processes, in contrast, are the ones that help skilled staff get more done. His company concentrates on creating good processes that offer just enough structure without imposing unnecessary layers of bureaucracy.

Several of the leaders I spoke with, work at companies that have created good processes that guide projects without stifling creativity. A number of the others bemoaned the lack of such a framework at their company. There was agreement across most of these folks that having a great, flexible all-purpose process is a good thing. These leaders know that teams that don't have a customizable process available to them will have to pause and create one from scratch at the start of each new project. Creating such a process is a waste of valuable brainpower that could have been spent working on the content of the project.

Is there a good all-purpose process that can offer just enough guidance and structure to meet the needs of massively different projects? Yes. It is Agile Methodology.

AGILE METHODOLOGY AS YOUR PROCESS

Agile was developed in the early 2000s as a framework to guide the work of software development groups. Because then, a few innovative companies have realized the value of Agile for teams and projects that have nothing to do with software. Some leaders in those companies have customized this methodology for broader use at their firms.

This is a great idea, and I have encouraged many companies to use Agile more broadly. Since then, a few have done so yet, there are not many resources available to guide the use of Agile in non-software projects. I would like to rectify that by devoting this chapter to the translation of Agile concepts for a broad array of projects across your company.

AGILE FUNDAMENTALS

Agile starts with four general values, which are known as "the Agile Manifesto."[3] I have adapted them for your use with non-software related projects.

1. Having real, ongoing collaboration with customers is more important than simply enforcing contracts in a rigid manner.
2. Having results that work is even more important than spending lots of time carefully documenting how those results were achieved.
3. Fixing problems is more important than sticking with the original plan.

4. Quality interactions between staff are even more impor-
    tant than sticking with rigid processes.

These are not simply nice-sounding platitudes to be hung on
a poster and promptly forgotten. These philosophies are meant to
guide how work actually gets done.

There are 12 "Agile Principles" that expand on the four values.[4]
Adapted for non-software projects, they are:

1. Our highest priority is to satisfy our customers by deliv-
    ering segments of work that move us toward our project
    goals.
2. We try to deliver small segments frequently and get
    feedback from customers to determine, as quickly as
    possible, if there's a need for any changes.
3. The primary measures of progress are that those seg-
    ments thrill customers and contribute to overall project
    success.
4. We are willing to change what we are delivering even
    late in the project if that helps to meet the customer's
    needs, as long as the costs of such changes are accept-
    able to all.
5. We involve motivated individuals, give them the sup-
    port they need, and trust them to get the job done.
6. We set the stage for those individuals and teams to work
    together throughout the project.
7. The most effective and efficient means of communica-
    tion and interaction will be used to ensure that the work
    is done right and the results are optimal.
8. Agile processes promote a pace of work that should be
    sustainable indefinitely.
9. Continuous attention to good design and content excel-
    lence enhances project results.
10. Simplicity is valued over complexity. The idea is to do
    the work as simply as possible while achieving the proj-
    ect's goals.

11. Teams are empowered in ways that make sense for this company and industry.
12. Every so often the project team reflects on how to be more effective. Then, it fine tunes its behaviors.

In my work with companies using Agile, I have developed other important tips for getting work done in an Agile environment.

- Create just enough structure to guide the project without imposing unnecessary constraints.
- Do just enough up-front planning to effectively launch the project.
- Use iterative processes to design and deliver the project in segments or pieces. (With an iterative approach, a small amount of work is performed, tested, and tweaked before proceeding with the next portion of work.)
- Conduct detailed planning right before you start working on each new segment to integrate lessons learned and changes made in previous segments.
- Involve customers and stakeholders in the project.
- Managers are mainly guides, coaches, and barrier-busters. Team members are empowered to make many decisions related to the work and are given sufficient information and context to allow them to make the right decisions.
- Foster a spirit more akin to *Apollo 13* than the ill-fated *Challenger* space shuttle (speaking up, listening, willing to share unpleasant information about things that aren't working).
- Generally, assign roles based on expertise while also fostering a willingness to pitch in to help others get the job done well.
- If the project's parameters change, evaluate them against time and cost constraints.
- Everyone should own accountability for the entire project, in addition to their portion of the work.

- Use regular, quick check-in meetings and other appropriate methods of interaction and communication.
- Perform the most critical and hardest work first.
- Openly share project information with any interested employees or customers.

UPFRONT PROJECT PLANNING

Some project management processes encourage a staff person to lay out detailed plans for the project before any work begins. That person creates goals for the project and uses those goals to spell out the objectives and detailed steps outlining how the work should be done to achieve those objectives. Then they estimate the staffing, financial, time, and other resources that will be needed to achieve the project's objectives to make this happen. Next, they determine what people will be involved in which parts of the project. Sometimes they even outline who is responsible for making what decisions. This detailed planning is based on the belief that having a very specific road map will help the project run smoother, minimize changes as the work proceeds, and constrain unnecessary costs.

Unfortunately, detailed, up-front planning like this can create more problems than it solves. It often does minimize changes as the work goes on, and that's the trouble. Planners usually cannot know enough about the project upfront to accurately estimate all those details. They do the best they can with what they know. But, as the project proceeds, the plan usually needs to be changed. If the up-front plan is treated as sacrosanct, then necessary changes are prevented from happening.

Agile projects put just enough detail in the up-front plan so that the project's sponsors and owners know what they are committing to. Project planners work with leaders to determine how the project will contribute to company-wide directions, the goals of the project, and a reasonable estimate of the people and other resources that are likely to be needed. Other details emerge in mini-planning sessions that kick off the work on each segment.

Instead of doing all the detailed planning on their own or with just a few others, the project planners create an agenda for a kick-off session. From that point on, planning is a team sport. The members of project teams are invited to this initial meeting along with the project's customers. Together they turn project goals into a Project Charter that outlines the scope, major work segments, deliverables, and people to be involved in that segment of work. They agree on metrics that will be used to measure success and they uncover opportunities and risks that need to be monitored.

During this initial meeting, participants hear important messages directly from leaders. They learn how this project helps the company and they engage in a dialogue that puts the work in context. This conversation leads team members to feel personal ownership of the project and its success. It also allows individuals to get to know others in ways that build trust, respect, and the desire to help others succeed.

User stories are a great tool to guide project work; they can be created in this initial kick-off meeting. User stories describe the desired end state of a project and specific elements within it. These stories are often created by customers and employees assigned to this project, working together. The amount of detail included in the stories varies depending on the complexity of the project and the newness of ideas involved. The customer starts by describing the problems that led to this project. Then they describe what success will look like for various aspects of the project. For a complex project in which staff will be innovating new ideas, the customer desires are usually drawn out in greater detail. Those details can be part of the same story or can be split into mini-stories.

While they are in the same room, the teams not only work out the plan for the whole project, they take some time to outline the work of their own teams within the project. Then they can negotiate what they think they will need from each other while they are face to face. This gives the project a much smoother start than is possible for projects in which each team does their own segment-level planning separately.

The group determines the order in which the work segments should be completed. One of the differences between Agile and other project-planning processes is that in Agile the toughest work with the highest risks is done first. Other processes often leave the hardest parts for later. Unfortunately, when the tough areas are finally tackled, previously unknown issues may arise that require work to be redone. In the Agile universe, the best way to reduce rework is to do the tough stuff first.

Other important aspects of the project can also be discussed in this kick-off session. For instance, if certain work needs to be done in a certain order. Other items to be discussed are specific to the needs of that project. A general principle of Agile is to keep procedures to a minimum, providing just enough structure to get the job done without unduly constraining employees.

INITIATING THE WORK

DETAILED PLANNING

Because Agile requires less up-front planning, there is a need for more planning at the start of each work segment. The people with the expertise to plan that segment effectively should be brought together to conduct that planning. If possible, customers should be included in these sessions.

The group decides what work components need to be completed as part of this segment, the priority of those components, and who will be involved. At this point, they also detail the budget and estimate how long it will take to do the work.

As part of this planning, the group develops the criteria they will use to determine when a piece of work will be considered complete and measure the quality at which that work needs to be done. If you are designing and manufacturing parts for an airplane you will want to ensure that your work is error-free. That level of perfection is not required when creating a software game. In general, Agile tries to be thorough and accurate while not going overboard or seeking perfection. But the desired level of quality should depend on the particular project.

If the work is complex and/or of a large volume, the segment is split into manageable pieces, because a core principle of Agile is that sections of work be delivered frequently. Rather than create one large segment that might take months to complete, that work should be split into sections called "sprints."

PERFORMING, TRACKING, AND COMMUNICATING ABOUT THE WORK

Once work begins on a sprint, no additional changes can be requested. Although the goal of Agile is to remain flexible to customer needs, at some point the plan needs to be stabilized in order to allow employees to complete their best work.

If complications arise during the work, ideally the budget and time estimates will remain fixed and the work will be adjusted as needed. Some of the planned work may be put on hold if problems are encountered in achieving it. That work may be resumed at a later point if possible or everyone may agree to drop that particular part of the project.

Another principle of Agile is that staff pitches in to help others even when a particular task is beyond one's usual job description. This can require a culture change at companies where staff hold rigidly to their role and consider it stepping on another's toes to reach out to help. In Agile cultures, employees are rewarded for stepping outside their formal roles when it benefits the project.

A number of tools are available to help manage and communicate the status of the work in Agile. They're often called "information radiators."[5] For instance, a task-board is a visual display of progress made by a team during a sprint. The board shows what is being worked on, progress, and any issues that have arisen. Another tool is a "burndown chart," which is a graph that represents work and time remaining. These tools are available to anyone who is interested in knowing how the project is going. The team should hide nothing from itself or from visitors. It confronts issues openly and directly.

At the conclusion of a sprint, the work produced during that period should be provided to the customer. Rather than just dropping it off and considering it completed, a dialogue then takes place. Customer feedback from that dialogue helps uncover any possible issues or desired changes. Although the work was closed to changes at the beginning of the sprint, alterations can be considered at this point if they will improve the project. One of the fundamental principles of Agile is that it is iterative and integrates lessons as work proceeds. Although this may slow progress a bit at times, the result will usually be a higher quality and more pleasing to the customer.

One leader explained, "If you design and build what the customer thinks they want before you begin the project, then you often design and build something that really isn't what they wanted. Through an iterative process, you pull out what the customer really wants that they cannot articulate up-front."

MEETINGS

STAND-UP MEETINGS

"Stand-up meetings" are a feature of the Agile framework. Team members are brought together on a regular basis to share progress they are making and resolve any issues. The frequency of these meetings depends on the needs of the specific work segment.

The meetings are designed to be quick check-ins and the concept of standing up is literal. With everyone standing, only crucial topics are discussed, encouraging team members to be efficient. Stand-up meetings often discuss the following kinds of open-ended questions:

- What have we accomplished since the last meeting?
- What problems are we having and where might we need help?

- ❍ What have we learned that might help others?
- ❍ What do we plan to achieve by the next meeting?
- ❍ What might we need to change, let go of, or accelerate?

Team members need to understand what others are working on and how it fits into the overall project. This will help staff make the right decisions on both small and large issues. These meetings are not intended to be status updates between the project owner and each participant. Instead, in a typical stand-up meeting you go around the room and everyone summarizes their work and answers questions. The group then decides if any changes are needed.

One of the goals of the stand-up meeting is to identify and fix failures earlier in the process. Achieving this goal depends on a culture of openness in which it is appropriate to speak freely about things that are not working well. There should be no sacred cows or undiscussables in these meetings.

In the words of one leader, "In an Agile environment where you hire smart people, they assume expertise in others and don't start from a cynical place where they are judging others negatively. They recognize what others can contribute and listen to those other ideas."

RETROSPECTIVES

Every so often, either when work segments are completed or at big milestones, Agile brings together all the employees working on the project and their customers. They examine how the work is going, and identify improvements they want to make as they move forward. This is known as a retrospective meeting.

This is not intended to be a "blamestorming" session; there is a delicate balance between speaking up on tough subjects and recreational whining. Because it's often a fine line, you may want to have these meetings run by trained facilitators who are experienced in discerning that difference and can help attendees accomplish these goals.

MANAGEMENT ROLE

Managers play an important role in Agile; it is different than the role they play in other kinds of projects. One leader with whom I spoke affirmed: "There is a strong role for the manager. But it is not so highly prescribed that it looks exactly the same in all companies or even across different projects in the same firm." For instance, in some project teams, the leader facilitates the stand-up meetings. In other teams she or he sits back and encourages others to take that role. It depends on the style of the leader and the culture of the team.

The following list summarizes some of the more important roles for managers in Agile projects. [6]

- ◗ Hire and retain great employees who are motivated to grow their expertise and do the best they can.
- ◗ Provide a connection between organizational direction and current projects. Do this regularly, not just at the initiation of a project. Provide the context that enables employees to make appropriate decisions at their level.
- ◗ Partner with the team to create inspiring goals for the project.
- ◗ Create an environment that promotes continuous learning and growth. Host learning sessions and recognize employees who learn on their own.
- ◗ Create an open, transparent environment.
- ◗ Support teams in problem identification and solving, and teach employees how to fix problems more effectively. The teaching role is key, because it helps employees learn how to fix the problems themselves rather than doing it for them.
- ◗ Remove barriers standing in the way of employees doing better work.
- ◗ Be available to staff when needed, without doing the work for them.

- Help determine and obtain the resources that enable the team to do their best, and that reflect organizational commitment to this project.
- Build partnerships with others in the company. Reinforce the right level of connection with other teams.
- Protect the team from unnecessary distractions.
- Be a career coach and advisor for employees, assisting them in ongoing professional development. Provide performance feedback and rewards that encourage employees to do their best and that reinforce appropriate career paths for each individual.

The difference between the managerial role in Agile and in other project management methods is that in Agile, managers are no longer assumed to be *the* one and only project sponsor or owner. It is their job to ensure that employees understand how they are contributing to overall company goals and continue to provide information and set the context throughout the project. It is also their job to partner with employees working on the project to maintain crucial relationships with others teams. Additionally, it's their job to retain great employees by continuing to work with them on career goals. It is also their job to work with employees who are underperforming or otherwise not contributing to project progress.

(Management roles in collaborative environments will be discussed further in Chapter 10.)

MANAGING SCOPE CREEP

"Scope creep," for those who might not be familiar with the term, refers to continual expansion of project goals through uncontrolled growth and by adding work that was not part of the initial scope of the project.

Because Agile defines fewer details of a project in up-front planning and because it has a philosophy of remaining open to appropriate change as the project proceeds, some fear that this project management methodology leaves it more open to inappropriate scope creep than other processes. The crucial distinction hinges on the definition of "inappropriate."

Imagine that your team is producing your company's next version of a highly popular, low-priced digital camera. Suddenly a competitor introduces a camera with picture clarity that is much better than yours. As soon as this becomes known, some staff panic. They feel that the project teams should pause their work and determine how to increase the picture clarity of this camera so it will be competitive. They argue that if the camera is completed with the old specifications then nobody will buy it. It will be obsolete before it's even released.

Other employees argue that the changes would have to be massive and that because the work is so close to being completed (the camera is 90 percent complete) it doesn't make sense to integrate such a big, new goal at this point. They feel that the costs would be prohibitive and spell the failure of this project.

If teams are rewarded only for producing what they agreed to do up-front, at the cost that was estimated, then leaders will decide in favor of those who are resisting the changes. If teams are rewarded for producing what the company actually needs, then leaders will decide in accord with those who believe the project should be paused to come up with better picture clarity or some other improvement to give the camera a competitive edge over the one that's just been released. In Agile, it's much more likely that the latter will happen: that the project will be paused to determine how to make the camera better.

What makes Agile useful is not that it accepts all changes proposed at any point. It attempts to teach employees how to do trade-off analyses and how to make those tough decisions. Here are some tips for making those trade-off decisions[7]:

- ○ It is not scope creep if detailed planning has not yet begun.
- ○ It also is not scope creep if it creates no additional work.

- ❍ It is sometimes acceptable scope creep if these changes could not have been known at the start, and if the delivered product better meets expectations regarding what is needed.
- ❍ It is usually acceptable scope creep if those important changes fall within the "contingency allowance" that was set for the project.
- ❍ The ultimate goal is the integrity of the project.

 APPLICATION

Do you have an all-purpose process that can be customized to help guide and track work, especially in projects with any degree of complexity? Does your company separate high-level planning from detailed planning, doing just enough upfront planning to set the stage for the project without inappropriately tying the hands of employees? Does your company provide tools that enable interactions and communication between staff who need to work with others? Do you see the value of stand-up meetings and retrospectives for projects at your company? Do managers at your company take on roles similar to those outlined here? In what ways don't they? Do you think it would be more useful if they would?

THE TAKE AWAY

Agile is not anti-planning. Nor is it anti-documentation. Agile recognizes the need to capture how things are being done. It also recognizes that many project management processes make documentation one of the chief priorities. In doing this, they place capturing how things are being done above actually doing the work. This is not a good thing.

Leaders are sometimes concerned that Agile might not be applicable for larger projects. In practice, I have found that its flexibility allows the inclusion of as many or few project segments and work groups as are needed.

Agile is also accused, at times, of being undisciplined and lacking accountability for project results. The short, defined sprints with distinct deliverables counter that complaint.

Agile is not a magic bullet. It doesn't fix all the problems that other project management methodologies encounter. It has plusses and minuses as well. It doesn't anticipate or provide everything you need for every project, but it is a useful tool for project management across a wide array of projects that a company undertakes.

9

OTHER VITAL TEAM TOOLS THAT BOOST COLLABORATION

People with different expertise and backgrounds see the world differently.

As one Silicon Valley leader said, "When you are bringing people together who have different competencies, they think and act differently. Their brains are wired differently. For example, marketing and finance were working together recently. The two departments' spreadsheets didn't even look alike."

Other leaders said similar things. As one put it, "Operations and product groups see the world differently." Another summed it up as: "It's as if we're all roped together, climbing up the mountain, and we each think we have a better path up that mountain. We all have the same goal, but we're all tugging to get others to follow *our* path."

You probably aren't surprised to hear that people with different perspectives see the world differently. We often wish that this wasn't the case. We wish that people could always work together seamlessly.

You might assume that things are different at companies that boast great collaboration, that folks at those companies work well together right from the start. In reality, Silicon Valley leaders have not stopped these differences in perspective from occurring. Nor do they want to. They know, as one leader put it, that "conflict isn't necessarily bad. It's fine as long as it's done in a good way. Working successfully together isn't just about mindshare and liking each other. It's about mining the differences."

The leaders with whom I spoke shared the following ideas for helping employees with disparate views to work together well:

- ◐ "We make sure that all the groups working together on a project have shared goals. We don't want them cancelling others' efforts and wasting energy working against each other."

- ◐ "In the past, when we saw an opportunity we jumped on it. Now we pause and remind ourselves of our overall strategy. We make sure that this new direction will help us achieve our strategy. We find ways for staff to 'hold that strategy in their hand' so they can judge whether this new opportunity is on or off target. It democratizes the reason, the why."

- ◐ "We take time to set context. We anticipate differences and help work through them."

- ◐ "We've found that most difficulties aren't usually because of content differences. Much more frequently, they are based on styles and approaches. We supply tools to help staff work together better."

Let's take a closer look at how one company helps set the tone for employees to work together. What follows is a description of a unique program they use to bring employees together.

HOW SANDISK INCREASES TEAM EFFECTIVENESS

We are immensely grateful to our global sales force at SanDisk. They work extremely hard and only come together as a whole team once or twice a year. They use those meetings to learn even more about our products, company goals, strategies, and progress. They also use the time to grow themselves as professionals and energize themselves for the next selling cycle. Their external clients often attend parts of the meeting.

This year, they decided to include a volunteer event as part of their meeting. They had done it before and found that it hugely enhanced employee work relationships. Although they hadn't included clients previously, they wanted to this time.

At SanDisk, we are deeply committed to philanthropy and helping communities in which we work. Our philanthropic programs have also become a way to strengthen our ability to work together across our teams. In working together on a meaningful volunteer activity, participants develop strong bonds. They feel honored to work side-by-side to make the community (or the world) a better place. When employees return to work, things are different. They have much stronger respect for each other. They realize that they truly are all part of a greater whole.

We helped the organizers of the sales meeting plan a volunteer event to assist a non-profit group whose goal is to eradicate hunger. It was a bit of a challenge to include 800 people, but it came together well. These 800 people worked side-by-side, packaging 450,000 meals to feed the hungry. They were so enthusiastic that many of them chose to go back to the warehouse on their own, to participate in the next steps in getting the food out to those who desperately need it.

As consistently happens, these 800 people went back to their meeting with very different attitudes. The rest of the meeting surpassed people's expectations in the ways that the participants interacted with each other and the decisions they made.

After these volunteer engagements, some of the most creative ideas come from the folks we least expect: employees who rarely spoke up before the event. The changes are so meaningful . . . almost magical. Staff risk sharing their ideas because nobody feels "dragged through the dirt." Even if their ideas aren't used, they know they were seriously considered. The trust developed while working together to help people in their communities creates the safety to work together to fix big hairy problems at work.

THE TAKE AWAY

For SanDisk, the positive effect of these volunteer activities is long lasting. Employees get to know each other while working on an issue of importance to the community, on which they see eye-to-eye. They learn about each other, their families, their hobbies, and their values. After they return to work, these new bonds create understanding, empathy, and a safety net for taking risks and sharing ideas that are not "wholly baked."

Using a volunteer program to help staff get to know and trust others at a deeper level may or may not work at your company. The take-away should be that respect and trust can foster a safe environment in which staff want to share and are willing to take the risk of expressing ideas that are not yet fully researched.

Although that environment can be built in many different ways, it needs to be built in order for people to work together well. As one leader of a large, well-known Silicon Valley company remarked, "Sharing your untested ideas will, by definition, make you feel vulnerable. You could have a radically new idea. If you don't feel safe, then you won't put it out. Organizations benefit when people are willing to think creatively and take the risk of sharing those ideas. That's a part of our culture here. Emotional safety lives here."

Your company needs to build that trust, respect, and sense of a safe environment.

APPLICATION

Think about the way SanDisk helps people get to know each other and build a culture of safety. Could that method work at your company? Does your company do things to help employees get to know others personally to build those bonds? How well does that work? Does there need to be more of this?

TOOLS THAT HELP GROUPS WORK MORE EFFECTIVELY

This chapter will offer two tools to assist groups of people in becoming more effective. The first one, Framing Topics, helps narrow a group's focus so that they don't waste time considering a variety of subjects that add no value to the conversation. The second one, Scenario Planning, a structured way of thinking about the future, is a tool for situations when you need to take into account aspects of the future that are unpredictable. We often see uncertainty about the future as a problem to either be immediately solved or ignored. Scenario Planning helps us see uncertainty as an opportunity rather than a problem to be minimized.

FRAMING TOPICS

What does it mean to frame a topic? Taken literally, a frame is a border that separates something from its surrounding environment. In the same way that a picture frame helps to focus our eye on the enclosed art piece, framing can do the same for a conversation. It focuses our attention on a particular aspect of a topic.

You're probably familiar with the saying "garbage in, garbage out." It arose with the advent of computers, and made people aware that if you put the wrong information into a system, the wrong information will result. If we are unclear about what we are doing in a particular meeting or even an entire project, we're not likely to achieve the result we desire. Albert Einstein supposedly said, "If I had an hour to solve a problem and my life depended on the solution, I would spend the first 55 minutes determining the proper question to ask."[1]

Imagine a group of people coming together to discuss how to improve employee satisfaction. If those three words (*improving employee satisfaction*) were the only introduction to the topic, you might observe the dialogue jumping from salaries to vacation policy to sick leave to bonuses. Although any of those topics might bring out some interesting points, they will be of little benefit if the purpose of the discussion was to focus specifically on the company's work-at-home policy.

If the person calling the meeting had let attendees know that the purpose of the meeting was to explore the specific sub-topic of employee requests to work at home, then participants would have arrived ready to talk about it. The conversation probably wouldn't have wandered into those other areas. If it had, the facilitator or a coworker could have redirected them back to the intended focus.

How many times have you sat in a meeting and realized after 20 minutes that the conversation has wandered way off topic? If the meeting organizer "frames" the topic carefully and with forethought, this is less likely to happen.

Framing is not only useful in setting the agenda and introducing the topic, it continues to be useful throughout the conversation. And it is a useful tool for everyone—not just the meeting organizer or facilitator. Effective collaboration is much more likely when attendees take ownership of the task of guiding the conversation to the right places.

What follows are four categories that can help frame a conversation and help participants focus on the right topics.

THE FOUR WHAT'S

Think of your conversation in terms of:

- ○ *What Is.* The facts and evidence we know about this topic.

> ◗ *What Should*. The opinions, views, and judgments we
>   need to know more about.
> ◗ *What If*. Brainstorming possibilities and new ideas
>   regarding the topic.
> ◗ *What Then*. Where we want to take this topic. How we
>   wrap it up for today and set up the next steps.

I will share tips in the following section for using these Four What's effectively, as well as offering several other categories of thought to assist you in framing your discussions.

ASKING THE RIGHT QUESTIONS

There is an art to framing topics in ways that brings out individual intelligence and weaves it into a communal brain. Asking questions is particularly useful. "Questions stimulate the mind and offer people an opportunity to use their brains [even more] constructively."[2]

As an experiment, when you want to engage others, phrase what you want to say in the form of a statement. Then observe what happens. Did it result in the conversation you were hoping for? The next time, try articulating your thought in the form of a question. What happened this time?

For example, regarding your company's work-at-home policy, if you are wording your thought as a statement, you might say, "Our company's policy regarding work at home is too restrictive. It needs to be more flexible and allow more employees to take advantage of it." If you are wording it as a question you might say, "What effect do we think our company's work-at-home policy has on employee satisfaction, and the decision that some of them make to leave our company?"

Beginning the conversation with a question can set the tone so that the ensuing discussion is collaborative, whereas starting with a statement can polarize others who disagree with your statement and create more of a debate environment.

What follows are brief summaries of major types of questions that are useful in setting up various kinds of collaborative discussions. (Four of the seven types of questions are from the Four What's. I have added three other types of questions.)

- ◗ *Questions that help determine the needed focus of a discussion.* What seems to be the problem? For whom is it a problem? In what ways are things going particularly well? If we were going to improve two to three things, which would be highest priority?

- ◗ *Questions that elicit detail when people do not understand a topic.* These questions are often called "funnel" questions because they start at a general level and guide folks to a more specific place as their understanding increases. Useful questions in this category include: Can you tell us more about the issue? What did you like about it? What confused you? What could you have used more or less of? What are the most important lessons from that situation?

- ◗ *Questions to guide a group toward a vision (to help explore "What If" topics).* What about this situation do we most care about? What does this mean for us? What about this would inspire us? How would we like this to be? What would be the ideal? How could we move toward that ideal? If we could ask a clairvoyant three questions about this situation what would they be? How would we answer those questions?

- ◗ *Questions to help consider alternatives and options.* What should be our criteria for judging these ideas? On what should we base our decisions? Based on those criteria do any ideas seem stronger than others? Do any seem weaker? How might we best meet our goals? What other issues might we want to consider? How might this change the way others are thinking or working?

- ◗ *Questions that elicit data (to help explore "What Is").* What evidence do we have to support that thought? Should we gather more information on this topic? What else do we need? Who might be willing to do that research and bring it to our next meeting?

○ *Questions to surface opinions, judgments, assumptions (to help explore "What Should" issues).* What are you hearing about this situation? What do you observe? What do you think about this? What do you feel about it? How should we interpret it? What thinking (and assumptions) might support those notions? What important events from the past should we recall as we plan this topic?

○ *Questions to move to action (to help explore "What Then" topics).* How should we complete this project? What steps should we take? Who needs to be involved? Who needs to be informed? Who should be performing which tasks? What are the timelines for these steps? How should we measure our effectiveness?

Do you notice the absence of a particular word among the sample queries provided here? Take a moment to glance back and see if you can guess. That missing word is *why*. Perhaps you have heard that "why" questions can be dangerous because they can sound judgmental and put people on the defensive. Still, there are times when "why" questions are called for. They can increase your understanding in totally different ways than questions of which, when, where, and how. Just be careful when you use the word *why* so the wording of the question and your tone of voice do not give the impression of an inquisition.

An example of a great use of "why" questions is "The Five Why's." This is a quick and effective process to help a group dig deeper to find root causes. After exploring a sub-topic, the question "Why?" is posed. When this is done five times, it can lead the group to great new realizations. Say you want to figure out why customers are suddenly returning so many women's blouses that they purchased from your company. You open the discussion with the first question and go from there.

1. Why are so many blouses being returned?
    Because too many buttons are falling off.
2. Why are so many buttons falling off?
    Because the sizing is wrong and many women are buying blouses one size too small. When they wear the blouse the buttons tend to pop off.
3. Why is the sizing wrong?
    Because we bought the blouses from a manufacturer in a different country that uses a different sizing system.
4. Why wasn't that detected before we bought the blouses?
    Because we usually only buy from the same manufacturers and know their sizing. It didn't occur to us to check this issue with the new manufacturer.
5. Why are we buying from a new manufacturer? Is that something we will do more often? Should we create a practice of checking sizing when we are working with new manufacturers?

THE TAKE AWAY

We often assume that questions are most useful for conversations in which we are brainstorming new ideas. But they can be used effectively for other purposes as well. They can be used to help:

- Persuade people.
- Gain information.
- Clear up fuzzy thinking.
- Motivate employees.
- Solve problems.
- Take the sting out of criticism.
- Overcome objections.
- Clarify instructions.
- Reduce anxiety.
- Defuse volatile situations.[3]

The effectiveness of questions depends on how they are framed. The key is making sure they are worded accurately to solicit the information you seek. Their effectiveness also depends on authenticity. Are they being used to genuinely explore? If so, then they will likely be met with openness and result in a successful conversation. However, if someone is using questions to manipulate a conversation, then others will probably notice this and the dialogue will be unsuccessful. It may even impair the trust others have in the asker beyond this one conversation.

One Silicon Valley leader offered a great tool that he has used over the years. One or more participants in a meeting are dubbed the "rat-hole patrol." They are armed with humorous cards with a picture of a rat in a hole. When the group goes off focus, a member of the rat-hole patrol throws a card on the table; one that looks like this:

Graphic by Eileen Zornow

 APPLICATION

Do employees at your company frame topics appropriately? How would you rate your firm on this skill? Try some of the skills provided in this section.

SCENARIO PLANNING

Desired futures don't just happen, they are created. Creating those great futures means that we have to consider uncertainties and do a better job of predicting what will happen. Predicting the future used to mean doing accounting-like forecasts. Employees told themselves that if something had been true in the past and is true in the present, then it's logical to assume it will still be true in the future. The problem is that this type of thinking doesn't allow us to factor in possible changes.

Scenario Planning can help guide decisions when a team is facing significant uncertainties. By using the data we have and combining it with our observations and well-founded perceptions, we can make reasonable guestimates about how things might unfold. We are not betting on one particular future. Instead, the idea is to create several scenarios that describe how things might play out. Then we make a decision that provides the most promise for as many of these scenarios as possible.

Peter Schwartz, a noted American futurist and author, was instrumental in shaping Scenario Planning.[4] The process that follows is one that I customized over the years in my work with companies. First, I will explain the eight-step Scenario Planning process. Then I will provide you with an example of how it works.

AN APPROACH FOR USING SCENARIO PLANNING

Step 1: Identify the issue under discussion. Take enough time to "frame" it carefully to ensure that you are working on the specific issue of concern. Also, be sure to enumerate how far into the future are you are considering. Two years? Five years?

Step 2: Identify the most important factors and trends that will be relevant to this decision over the time period of interest.

- These might include factors internal to the organization, such as the primary competencies staff currently have (or lack), your current products, and other factors that could influence your decision.

- ❍ It should also include factors external to the organization that are important to this issue, such as changing consumer preferences, competition, new technology becoming available, governmental regulations, and so on.

These factors and trends will be used to help create the scenarios. Typically, most of these factors are not subject to company influence in the short term.

Step 3: Examine the factors identified in Step 2 and determine whether or not each is highly certain to occur.

- ❍ Bucket all of the uncertainties together. These uncertainties will be used to craft the scenarios in Step 5. Then, prioritize these uncertainties. Which are most relevant to this project and the decisions you are making?
- ❍ Bucket the certainties together. These are essentially unchangeable pieces because they are highly likely to occur and there is not much you can do to influence whether they do or not. These are the fixed constraints that will help you examine your scenarios. Prioritize the certainties; you will use the most relevant ones to consider your scenarios.

Because of the importance of these two buckets, after you have assigned every factor or trend to one of the two buckets and determined the highest priority ones, double-check the high-priority items. What evidence supports your inclusion of that factor? Does it hold up to examination? What assumptions might you want to check out? This double-check increases the accuracy of your Scenario Planning process.

Step 4: Answer these questions to further increase the validity of the scenarios you will create.

- ❍ Is there anything else that happened in the past or is happening now that might shape the future related to this subject?

- **◑** What haven't you been looking at that you should consider?

Step 5: Now it is time to bring together the high-priority uncertainties into four scenarios, each of which summarizes how the future may look with respect to this issue.

- **◑** You should craft the four scenarios so they contain some variation of the high-priority uncertainties. This may sound confusing in abstract terms, but it should become clearer when you see the following example on page 163.
- **◑** Four scenarios are suggested so the group will give due consideration to each scenario rather than taking the easy way out and concentrating mainly on the middle scenario. The objective is to reach a solution or decision that is best for all of these scenarios, not just one them.
- **◑** Insert the most important certainties into the scenarios as constraints. (They remain the same across each of the scenarios.) Again, this should be clearer when you see it demonstrated in the following examples.

Step 6: Step back from the four scenarios and assess them. The following questions can be used to check them for usefulness:

- **◑** Does this scenario make logical sense?
- **◑** What chain of events could lead to this future? Is it plausible?

Based on your answers to these questions, you may want to revise some of your scenarios or create new ones.

Step 7: Examine the decision you are trying to make in relation to these scenarios. The goal is to make a decision with the greatest potential for success across all of these possible futures because you don't know which one will come about. An important question to ask is: What decision would allow us to the best chances of being successful, regardless which of these four scenarios actually happens?

Step 8: Select your final decision and formulate an implementation plan for executing it. You may want to include a "yellow-light" warning system that requires you to reexamine your decision if conditions change and your scenarios are no longer accurate.

AN EXAMPLE OF SCENARIO PLANNING

To clarify how this works, here is a fictitious example of Scenario Planning applied by a company that is thinking of moving into the production of all-electric vehicles. (This example is not based on real data. It is a simplified version of what you might create when using this process with a real issue.)

Step 1: Framing the issue: Can we base a lucrative business around manufacturing and selling all-electric vehicles in five years?

Step 2: Sample trends relevant to this decision: (You should create an exhaustive list of important factors and trends well beyond this abbreviated example.)

- Price of gasoline in five years.
- Availability of public charging stations for all-electric vehicles.
- Cost of public charging stations for all-electric vehicles.
- The feasibility of having a private charging station at one's home.

Step 3: The first three bulleted trends in Step 2 are uncertainties. We do not know what the situation will look like with respect to any of these three issues in five years. The fourth trend will be considered a certainty for this scenario. We are going to assume that anyone purchasing an all-electric vehicle will want and be able to have a charging station at their home.

- ◗ We bucket together the first three bulleted trends as uncertainties, and identify all of them as highly relevant for this example.
- ◗ We have one certainty for this example. It too is considered highly relevant.
- ◗ A double-check of these four trends supports their inclusion and their placement in the buckets mentioned previously. (If this had been real, we would have conducted research to check out the validity of assumptions we were making with these four factors.)

Step 4: When we ask ourselves the two questions posed in Step 4, we find that the four trends that we identified sufficiently cover the important issues. No other factors or trends are identified.

Step 5: Here are the four scenarios:

- ◗ *Scenario 1*: The price of gas is considerably more expensive in five years. Public car charging stations are widely available at freeway exits and on local roads at a very low cost for customers. Private charging stations are widely available and affordable at people's homes.
- ◗ *Scenario 2*: The price of gas is somewhat more expensive in five years. Public car charging stations are widely available at freeway exits but not on local roads. Charging stations are of moderate cost for customers. Private charging stations are widely available and affordable at people's homes.
- ◗ *Scenario 3*: The price of gas costs about the same in five years as it does today. Public car charging stations are of limited availability at freeway exits and on local roads. Those charging stations are high cost for customers. Private charging stations are widely available and affordable at people's homes.

- *Scenario 4*: The price of gas is less expensive in five years than it is today. Public car charging stations are not readily available at freeway exits or on local roads. Those charging stations are very high cost for customers. Private charging stations are widely available and affordable at people's homes.

Step 6: In conducting the check of the four scenarios each seems logical, plausible, and useful as written.

Step 7: Now it's time to consider our decision in light of these scenarios. The decision is whether to move to the manufacturing and selling of all-electric vehicles in five years. Considering this in relation to each of the four scenarios we come to the following:

- *Scenario 1*: After estimating costs, benefits, and limitations we conclude we should definitely move to manufacturing and selling all-electric vehicles under the circumstances enumerated within this scenario.
- *Scenario 2*: After estimating costs, benefits, and limitations we conclude that we should move to manufacturing and selling all-electric vehicles under these circumstances as well.
- *Scenario 3*: After estimating costs, benefits, and limitations we come to the conclusion that we should move to manufacturing and selling all-electric vehicles under these circumstances. The demand for these vehicles will be such that our profit will be less but still high enough to warrant this move, under the circumstances we have outlined in the third scenario.
- *Scenario 4*: After estimating costs, benefits, and limitations we come to the conclusion that we should not move to manufacturing and selling all-electric vehicles under these circumstances. The demand for an all-electric vehicle will be so much lower if these

circumstances come about that our profits would be insufficient. Under this scenario we could not base a lucrative business around manufacturing and selling all-electric vehicles in five years.

Step 8: Our Scenario Planning activity gives us confidence to move ahead with our decision to manufacture and sell all-electric vehicles because three of the four scenarios tell us that this strategy can be profitable. However, because one scenario indicates otherwise, we will continue to monitor these factors, and if any of them seem to be moving in unfavorable directions, we will reconsider our decision.

Scenario Planning is a way to bring as much intelligence as you can to a highly ambiguous situation. It helps you consider uncertain futures and make decisions with some rigor. The Scenario Planning process takes time. It is not intended for relatively easy decisions and it should be reserved for decisions in which a lot is at stake.

 APPLICATION

Could Scenario Planning help structure some of your own discussions on topics that are enmeshed in uncertainty because of unknowns about the future? Consider trying it out when you are planning a meeting to discuss a complex topic.

This eight-step process should be sufficient to plan and implement use of Scenario Planning. If you would like additional information, I highly recommend Peter Schwartz's book, *The Art of the Long View.*

10

ARCHITECTING YOUR MANAGEMENT PRACTICES

This chapter will focus on the first of three Company Practices that help foster collaboration: the role of management. First, I will share some insights of Silicon Valley leaders on various aspects of people management. After that, I will offer a number of tips regarding particular management practices.

Let's start with a story that illustrates how important management decisions are when it comes to creating effective collaboration.

AN EXAMPLE OF HOW FORCED SEPARATION UNDERMINES COLLABORATION

I previously worked at a well-known company in Silicon Valley that produced mobile communication devices and the software that ran those devices. After much consideration, executives of this company made the difficult decision to sequester employees working on the physical device from those working on the software. It was only done because some of our customers demanded it.

Some of those customers wanted to purchase our physical device and operate it with software from other companies. Others wanted to use our software on physical devices sold by other companies. Each of those sets of customers was customizing our products to work differently with products from our competitors. They were concerned that we could gain an unfair advantage if we used information about how they were customizing our product to work with products offered by our rivals. In order to appease their concerns, our leaders agreed to separate our two groups into discrete divisions that had very limited communication with others.

Employees worked very well with others in their division, but did not collaborate with colleagues in the other division. In fact, the separation was so effective that very few employees at any level of this company understood the details of both products.

This caused serious problems. Staff in the physical device division would contact software employees and say, "We need you to do X with the software." The software folks would push back, saying they couldn't do it for a variety of reasons that they were not at liberty to explain. The same happened in reverse. The software folks made requests of the device employees, which that group said they were unable to meet. This resulted in stalemates.

Eventually issues would bubble up three or four levels until someone finally made a decision. Often those decisions were better for the customer than for our company. Because of our decision to partition, we were not benefitting from producing both software and hardware related to the same device. In fact, we had less influence between our two areas than outside companies had with us.

Every company that is faced with dilemmas of this nature has to figure out what the best decision is for their unique circumstances. There is not one clear-cut answer that is right for everyone in this situation. For us, the right decision was to relax the separation between the divisions. We realized that isolating the two divisions from each other didn't make good business sense for us. We let our customers know why we had to make this change. And we made it.

Things didn't improve immediately when we brought the two divisions back together. Sequestering them had been so effective that it took quite a bit of work to reverse. Even though employees bought into the notion of collaboration and did it very effectively within their division, the walls between the two groups had caused enormous rifts that had to be actively mended.

We hosted a number of workshops to increase collaboration between the two divisions. We emphasized how we needed the two groups to work together. Management modeled how to collaborate with colleagues in the other division. Over time, the walls came down and employees began collaborating as well across the divisions as they had been doing within their own division.

THE TAKE-AWAY

This story is an all-too-real example of a strategy that not only hurt collaboration, but also hurt the company's profitability. Clearly, executives knew that this strategy would keep employees from working together. For a period of time, though, they thought it was worthwhile financially to do it.

Sometimes it's hard for management to see that a certain policy or practice is bad for collaboration and the company's bottom line. In some cases, the problems are visible to employees long before management realizes their damaging effects. Not only do leaders need to actively look for such situations, they should ask employees to let them know if they notice this happening.

 APPLICATION

Does your firm have any strategies or practices that make sense from certain perspectives, yet have a negative impact on successful collaboration? Are leaders aware of how damaging these practices are?

Now that we've seen how important management practices are to collaboration and company success, I would like to share some insights on effective managerial practices that Silicon Valley leaders relayed to me. As you read, think about which of these are relevant to your company.

MANAGEMENT PHILOSOPHIES SET THE STAGE

- ○ "Since our new CEO joined the company several years ago, we have a new philosophy. He inspires us to see that we're truly all one team. Before he arrived, each division did their own thing. There was no central glue. Things were not only not collaborative, they were adversarial. He's changed it tremendously. We now have a 'Customer First' philosophy that brings us all together. We are able to create shared goals for projects. It helps us work together rather than working against each other."

- ○ "This company has spent the last three to four years evolving from a company that makes and sells certain products for money, to being a company that centers on our customers. This was an executive decision made a few years ago. We make sure that everything we do is best for our customers. This helps us be more empathetic to customers. It also helps us to have greater empathy for other staff. Both are very good things."

- ○ "Jesus, Lao Tzu, and other famous leaders throughout history have helped us to see that telling people what to do (and pushing them to do it) isn't nearly as powerful as guiding others to reach those conclusions themselves. These leaders were right. You don't build a great boat just by building it. You do it by inspiring folks to want to go to sea. You do it by connecting the mission of the company with the work that individuals do."

- ● "Collaboration is 'context over control.' That means we're not trying to force a particular perspective or a prescription for how things have to be done. Instead, we set context. We have this business goal and this need. How do we work together to achieve it?"

- ● "Leaders need to set context in ways that make sense to a diverse staff who have very different styles. Looking across an organization, you see a lot of left- and right-brained folks. You need to make things meaningful to all of them. Our great leaders do that. They share both the facts and the inspirational stories that engage us emotionally. And state things in several different ways to engage everyone."

VALUES: "OUR MANAGERS CARE DEEPLY AND SHOW IT"

- ● "Our managers care deeply. They care about staff as well as the organization's purpose. They do their best to set teams up to succeed. Then, they delegate the work with high expectations. It works."

- ● "Our CTO [chief technical officer] taught me ways to build trust quicker. How to walk in another person's shoes. Some are surprised that I learned these soft skills from a CTO. This man has superb emotional intelligence as well as technical chops."

- ● "Leadership sets the tone for how teams interact. If you have an obstructionist leader, that sets a negative tone. This company has a collaboratively driven leadership team. It's genuine, not forced or make-believe. Not working well together is just not tolerated. The executive leadership team works very closely as a team. They work really well with the next level of management. And so on. It sets the tone for all of us."

- ● "One interviewee demonstrated a crucial lesson. She instructed me to make an 'ok' symbol with my thumb and index finger. 'Now,' she told me, 'touch your chin with those fingers while making that symbol.' As she spoke, she demonstrated visually. But, as she told me to touch my chin she touched her cheek. I did the same. She summarized the lesson. 'What leaders do is even more influential than what they say. If the two conflict, people put more weight in actions than in words.' "

CREATING INSPIRING VISIONS: "WE COULDN'T WAIT TO GET HIS VOICEMAILS"

- ◖ "The executives at my previous employer were inspiring. They could conjure up an image and make it live in people's brains. They were amazing story-tellers. They used metaphors, talked about what was important to them personally, and connected stories to our core values."

- ◖ "One of my favorite bosses had a wonderful way of communicating. He didn't just talk with us once a quarter to announce results. He put out a Friday morning voicemail message. During one six-month period, he related our work to the building of the Brooklyn Bridge. ('If you think you have a tough job, think of what was required of those bridge builders.') We couldn't wait to get his next Friday voicemail."

- ◖ "One of our executive's key messages was: 'Team up, you cannot get this job done by yourself.' He urged people to work together and keep trying."

- ◖ "He shared so much about himself that you felt you knew the guy. That made us much more committed to him and to the company."

- ◖ "She didn't beat people up. She did whatever was needed to support employees. She still held us accountable, respectfully. And we loved that."

PRACTICES: "WE SHIFTED FROM AN ANSWER ECONOMY TO A QUESTION ECONOMY"

- ◉ "It's about building alliances across the organization to get the best out of everyone. We work together across disciplines to get things done."
- ◉ "It starts with everyone on a project having shared goals. When different groups have conflicting goals, all they do is work against each other."
- ◉ "Managers at my company used to tell employees what to do, what to think, and how to do their work. Then they learned to ask questions and let others come up with the answers. Now, they have an even more effective style. Folks take ownership for both asking the questions and finding the answers to well-articulated, thoughtful questions. The greatest innovations come from the right questions. We have shifted from an answer economy to a question economy."
- ◉ "We know things work much better if we inspire and involve than if we impose. It works. We have gone from 14 percent employee involvement to 92 percent. That's made a big difference to employees. And managers too. Problems that we thought were intractable aren't intractable at all."
- ◉ "Leaders sometimes need to say 'We have to do this.' We have a positive history built now, so when that happens, folks are okay with it. They understand and say let's get it done and move on."
- ◉ "I make sure my teams have information. I constantly try to provide context."
- ◉ "I protect my teams. I keep the politics and noise away from them so they can do a great job. I'm the filter, sending the things through that they need and keeping the rest out."
- ◉ "I was sure that mentoring and coaching your team and growing your people would not change in an Agile

environment. But it did change, hugely. Previously, we thought we were enlightened managers. But we really weren't. We had little time to coach and grow folks. Agile gives me the space to do those things because the whole team owns the product. My role is to support employees and enable them to create that product at whatever quality is needed."

- ○ "You have to care in a different way. Managers need to really understand team work and effectiveness and value the principles of Agile. Not just do Agile, but be Agile."

- ○ "Managers become facilitators of the team's work. We become leaders rather than directors or delegators."

- ○ Yes, we still have hierarchies, but we've removed the barriers between groups. Managers have changed from directing individuals and functions to leading teams."

- ○ "As a leader, it's no longer our job to say 'Go do this.' It's more about 'Here's where we are going, how do we get there, what might get in our way, and what we should we do about it?' Seek that input and discussion."

- ○ "I have worked in command-and-control-style companies. I just can't work in places like that anymore. I have a more collaborative style. I believe you get what you manage to. When employees come and ask me what they should do about something, I answer them with questions to get them thinking."

- ○ "I've never had or been a command-and-control manager. It's more, 'There are your priorities. How are you going to fulfill them?' Then you are evaluated against how you fulfill them."

- ○ "Sometimes staff who are having disagreements go to their manager and ask him or her to make the decision. Now it's more common for the manager to resist doing that, suggesting that they figure it out themselves. If it's really breaking down, then the manager will eventually step in."

- "Previously, it was top-down. If you happened to run over folks to get things done, the manager wouldn't call you on it. That doesn't fly today."
- "Accepting everyone's ideas all the time can lead to disastrous results. You end up with mediocrity. It's great to encourage new ideas. But there also needs to be a process to help the really good ideas flourish."
- "Leaders have to use persuasion power. If I am a product leader, I have to be able to convince folks that this idea is better than that one. They don't have to agree with me just because I'm their boss. I think this is quite healthy."
- "Managers now manage the quality of the effort. And they help their staff manage their careers. They assist folks in figuring out the next the career move, and what skills they will need in order to get there."
- "As a leader it is my responsibility to ensure we're focused on the right things. It's also my team's responsibility to notice those things and bring them to my attention. I see myself as a facilitator, hiring and bringing together a group of people that can do the job well."
- "I give folks the space to have private discussions with me; ones that stay private. They can have verbal diarrhea and we move on. Folks need a place to vent. And they need a sounding board to help them decide what to do about the tough stuff."
- "Our staff works hard, long hours. This is not unusual for start-ups. We don't have the luxury of a lull following intense periods of work so folks can relax a bit. We know this is unsustainable for the long term. Fortunately, employees are committed to our company. They understand how important it is for us to get a footing in the marketplace. We make it advantageous to them to indulge us this way."

- "We are still growing our management staff and helping them to learn. We're not perfect. But we realize what's important and are working on it."
- "Some of our leaders are able to delegate the work, trust staff, and let go. Others are still learning. They still get enmeshed in the details. They still micromanage. That's a bad thing. They are learning not to because it leaves folks feeling less empowered."

CORRECTIVE PRACTICES: COACHING NEW BEHAVIORS AND BEYOND

- "Resistance to change can work against getting better. I was at a company that wanted to implement big upgrades at a customer support center. The change would eventually make the work easier. But there was a lot to do to get there. There was incredible resistance. You heard, 'Everything is working. Why do we need to change it?' Finally, one manager decided he was going to champion the change. He drove it through. He wasn't autocratic. He sat down and explained why it was a good idea and people listened to him. After the fact, folks expressed how much they appreciated that he took that role and made the change happen."
- "It goes back to a story I heard from a management expert years ago. He used that children's story *Green Eggs and Ham* to describe the change process. 'The guy is chasing Sam I am, encouraging him to eat the green eggs and ham. Sam I am resists. Says he doesn't want it. The other fellow keeps trying to persuade him. Sam I am keeps resisting. . . . Finally, he's worn down and tries it. And loves it.' This can be your change management bible. You have to be persistent and consistent."
- "If folks try to dominate the conversation and don't accept feedback and change in response, they're eventually left off the team. We may bring them in as experts,

hear their ideas, ask questions, brainstorm with them. But they won't be permanent team members."

- ◐ "Regarding folks hoarding information, you just have to say, 'Look, that will not be tolerated. If you continue to do it, maybe there isn't a good fit for you in this organization.' That's a key part of management's job."
- ◐ "When it isn't working, sometimes we just have to let folks go."

 APPLICATION

Do you see the key themes running across these different examples: the management philosophies, values, inspirational practices, people-management strategies, and corrective practices that foster collaboration? Do you understand the way in which they create that collaborative culture? How closely do they match the management practices at your company? Do they offer any ideas for your organization?

SHARED GOALS ARE INDISPENSABLE

A number of Silicon Valley interviewees that I spoke with emphasized the importance of shared goals. A few of those comments were included in the previous excerpts.

Most employees in large organizations can give you an example of a time when conflicting goals between teams hindered them from being successful. For instance, one group believes in working on a product until there are virtually zero errors in it while another group places more importance on speedy delivery of the product to customers. Or the mismatched goals might be based on underlying differences in values.

Consider a case in which two groups work together to issue permits for new roads. One group values wider roads and narrower boulevards to aid traffic flow. The other places greater importance on wider boulevards and narrower streets for pedestrian appeal. If these two disparate goals are not sufficiently dealt with upfront, they can prevent the work from moving forward efficiently.

Sometimes the mismatched goals are set by leaders. When that's the case, employees need to bring the conflict to the attention of management as soon as it's realized. Quite often, managers will not be aware that they've created this problem. If there is a reason that those goals need to remain in place, then the leaders and staff can work together and figure out how to avoid the conflict.

At other times, mismatched goals are created by the groups themselves rather than being decided by management. When this happens, it's ideal if those groups can work it out between themselves. If that isn't possible then they need to involve leaders because it can thwart the project's success.

Having shared goals creates shared ownership and increases the willingness of groups to work together to find joint solutions. Shared goals between groups that need to work together is a start but isn't sufficient to ensure success in and of themselves. You need more. People also have to buy into the notion that they're all on the same team.

THERE IS NO PERFECT ORGANIZATIONAL STRUCTURE

Some people believe that the most effective solution to resolve collaboration problems is to require groups that need to work together to all report to the same manager. That solution is based on the belief that if groups are not working together well, then a common boss can require them to collaborate or solve the problems for them. But that's not a great solution, especially for companies that have more than a few hundred employees. When you are dealing with so many people it is physically impossible to have them all report to one person. It undermines the goal of managers having only as many direct reports as they can effectively coach and work with. It also undermines the notion of stable reporting relationships.

Let's consider the example of a product development project. Effective development usually involves bringing together employees from design, engineering, manufacturing, operations, sales, and marketing. If your company has a product-based organizational structure, then that structure could potentially allow all of the employees assigned to that project to report to one manager. But when a project is completed it is common for employees to be split up and moved to different projects. If your goal is to group employees that are working on a project under the same management, then you will have to continually change the reporting structure to adjust to those moves. That would impose instability on working relationships between employees and their manager. And still, that only works for the product development projects.

What about other part-time projects employees work on simultaneous with their product development work? Some of those employees might also be working on a project to redesign employee benefits. Other employees from that product development group might be assigned to a project to improve customer service. It is impossible to have all the employees working together on a project report to the same manager when employees work on multiple projects.

Almost every Silicon Valley leader I spoke with agreed that organizational structure cannot be the mechanism depended upon to resolve differences. Instead, the solution is to have a flatter organizational structure in which managers operate more as facilitators and coaches, and where leaders work together among themselves and with a host of groups to ensure that the work is accomplished. When this happens, then the inevitable challenges that arise can be mediated by the employees themselves or by managers that they might or might not report to.

SENIOR LEADERS OPERATING AS ONE UNIFIED TEAM

The top management team of a company needs to run the business together, rather than making decisions exclusively for their teams and lobbying for what will most benefit the groups they manage. When that top management team is indeed a primary team, working together to evaluate, make decisions, provide resources for, and sponsor key initiatives, they further the goals of the whole company. If instead, they are more concerned with maximizing the success of their own business unit, it will create a culture of adversity and internal competitiveness. And it will be impossible to get employees at lower levels to act differently.

 APPLICATION

Do groups working together in your organization usually have shared goals? Is there acknowledgment that your organizational structure will have both strengths and weaknesses when it comes to helping employees collaborate? Do your senior leaders work well together and with others, modeling successful collaboration right from the top? What you've learned in this chapter may provide additional evidence to help you to speak with leaders about making changes in your company's management practices.

11

EMPLOYEE INCENTIVES

This chapter will cover the second Company Practice that significantly affects collaboration: employee incentives.

The topic of employee incentives (how companies reward their employees for a job well done) is of utmost importance. As one Silicon Valley leader told me, "Behaviors flourish when they are rewarded."

Whereas management practices are quite consistent across the leaders I interviewed, the philosophies and approaches regarding employee incentives differ from company to company. Despite some differences in how they make this happen, many of the Silicon Valley leaders I spoke with choose to pay employees at the higher end of the pay range. They want to attract and keep highly experienced professionals. They also want their employees to have a comfortable lifestyle in the Bay area, a region with an extremely high cost of living. In return for paying them top dollar, most companies expect their employees to work very hard.

The following story, shared by a Silicon Valley leader, demonstrates a philosophy about employee incentives that is representative of many successful companies in the region, particularly the ones that foster employee collaboration.

IT BENEFITS YOUR COMPANY TO INCENT EVERYONE

At one point, I was involved in assimilating my company with another during a merger. One of the areas in which our two companies differed was the compensation system. The first company funded a pension for some leaders. It was restricted to a relatively small percentage of employees.

Our company (let's call it the second company) had a different philosophy regarding compensation. Our plan offered incentives to employees throughout the company. In addition to providing a reasonable salary, we offered bonuses to employees at all levels who exerted significant effort and achieved stellar results. We felt it was the right thing to do, to reward employees for their hard work. We also felt that doing so increased employee commitment, performance, and results, and contributed to the company's success.

We wanted the first company to move to our approach after the merger. Long discussions were held between our two companies. Leaders from the first company felt they couldn't afford to implement our plan because of the large number of employees at the combined new company. So, they felt there was no reason to debate whether our plan might provide more incentive for employees to work harder.

I knew that our plan (at the second company) was better. I spent a lot of time creating a business case to prove it. My goal was to show that the newly combined company could afford a plan like ours. It would just necessitate some re-prioritizing of rewards and other budget items. It took many conversations, but I was able to persuade executives that we could afford it. Once they saw enough evidence, they agreed that it was possible.

Next, I had to prove it was worth it. I had to show that sharing financial benefits with employees at all levels had more of a positive effect on company bottom line than just rewarding some leaders. I was able to collect that evidence from outside experts and their studies. With that data, I eventually convinced leaders of our combined company to adopt a rewards system that was broader and available to any employee who achieved high performance.

Most executives now strongly agree that this compensation system contributes to the company's overall bottom-line success.

THE TAKE AWAY

I firmly believe that there is no one single employee incentive system that is right across all industries or even within a specific industry. That being said, my experience corroborates the views of many Silicon Valley leaders and the studies demonstrating that rewarding all employees for hard work and achievements produces far greater benefits for a company than limiting rewards for high performance to executives.

REWARDING EMPLOYEES FOR GREAT WORK AND FOR WORKING TOGETHER

There was another crucial pattern running through the information that Silicon Valley leaders shared with me. Nearly every one of them recognizes how important it is to reward employees for working well with others. These firms not only create an expectation among their employees that they will collaborate with others, they build this expectation into their compensation systems.

Let's look at what some of those Silicon Valley leaders told me about their employee incentive programs, particularly as its relates to two areas: rewarding all employees for hard work and stellar results, and rewarding all employees for collaborating in ways that contribute to those results.

Different companies provide those rewards in different ways. Some do it through their basic salary/compensation systems. Others do it through bonuses. Still others do it through their benefit systems. What follows is a sampling of leader comments regarding how compensation is handled in their company. While reading, think about whether any of these ideas might be a good fit at your workplace.

COMPENSATION IS SIMPLE: PAY GREAT SALARIES FOR EXCELLENT PERFORMANCE

- ● "Compensation is simple: We pay top of market to every person based on their job. We look at how much they could they make at a different company. Then we factor in what it would cost to replace them. Ultimately, we ask ourselves how much we would pay to keep them if they said they were leaving."

- ● "Our philosophy is to take money off the table as an issue. In return, we expect employees to work hard. Not just for short dashes, but on an ongoing basis. Hard work is a way of life here. That said, though, we won't pay more than an employee can make elsewhere. We don't want to tie them to this company because of their pay check. We want them to be here because they're passionate about working for our company, and about what they are working on."

- ● "People are judged based on their technical contributions as well as their cultural fit (cultural fit includes factors such as how they work with others). Just because coworkers say great things about a person doesn't necessarily mean that they will get a lot more money. Employees only receive more money if they demonstrate performance, results, and an ability to collaborate."

- ● "We avoid 'top 30 percent' and 'bottom 10 percent rankings' of employees. In other words, we do not force-rank employees relative to their peers, because we don't want employees to compete. We want employees to help others, and they do. And we also want all of our employees to strive to be in the top 10 percent."

○ "Collaboration is one of the several objectives that staff are measured against here."

○ "We give managers a pot of money and let them decide how to distribute it within their team. We'll coach and guide them regarding the upsides and downsides of different strategies. (For example, if they give huge amounts to their top few employees, they're going to make most folks pretty unhappy.) We are moving towards a reward system that looks at what employees achieved and also how they achieved it. Whether they worked well with others. Whether they led the team when it was appropriate. Whether they helped move the company forward."

○ "Even at senior executive levels, we have strong financial reinforcement for collaboration. A significant portion of their review ratings and their compensation are based on how they work well as a team with their peers, as well as with other teams beyond the ones they manage."

BONUSES: A GREAT WAY TO REWARD COLLABORATION

○ "Bonuses here have well-thought-out performance criteria, including how we work with others and how well our company performs in the market during this time period."

○ "Bonuses are paid twice a year. They are based partly on company-wide factors (revenue, expense control, and profitability), and partly on business unit and individual results. How people work with others is factored into that second item."

○ "If someone rushes in at the last moment to save a project and we reward them, then everyone wants to become a hero. We try not to reward heroes. We try to reward those who work well with others on an ongoing basis and get the job done really well."

DEFERRED COMPENSATION CAN HAVE UNINTENDED EFFECTS

○ "We don't want managers to 'own' their people because of stock options and vesting. So all compensation is fully vested here. We want managers to create a great place to work. Employees are free to leave us at any time without penalty. But nearly everyone stays. Employees stay here because they like the company, they are passionate about their work, and because they are paid well for doing that work. Not because of a deferred compensation system."

VACATION: TAKE WHAT YOU NEED WHEN YOU NEED IT, AND RETURN REFRESHED

○ "We have open vacations here. People work hard. In return, they take the vacation they need to refresh. It's very odd if folks take less than three weeks. I'd be disappointed if they did take much less because they need that down time. It's usually between three to six weeks. Some years more, some less. My team has a very good rhythm. I've not had to ask anyone to be careful about vacations."

○ "We blew up our old vacation time accrual system. It works much better now. Highly tenured staff fought the change because they thought they were losing something, and that newbies were getting something that they didn't earn. I talked with them and challenged their (mis)perceptions. It was a hard sell. It took a while before folks realized that rewards should be based on doing your work well. Taking the day after Christmas off should not depend on your saving a vacation day from your annual allocation."

OTHER MEANINGFUL BENEFITS

- "We have up to one year paid for maternity. Not everyone takes nearly that long. People decide what they will take. However long they take, we prefer they unhook totally to give them time to adjust to parenthood (or parenting greater numbers of children)."
- "Recognition is really important, particularly among peers and coworkers. It has to be impartial. And those who get it need to be folks who really earned it. Or else it is pretty meaningless."
- "Recognition is strong here. People nominate others for having done something great. Anyone can recognize others. It encourages us to see the good things that others are doing, and take time to give them some kudos. It creates an atmosphere of collaboration. Next time we are working together, you remember that you are important to me and that I gave a tribute to what you did."
- "I recall being a member of one of those amazing groups. I have no recollection what I was paid at the time. The reward I got that was most meaningful to me was a handwritten note from the president. He just worked five doors away from me. And he took the time to deeply thank me, in writing. I still have that letter, and love it."

WHEN INCENTIVES ACT AS BARRIERS TO COLLABORATION

- "Differences in pay for the same job and equivalent performance make people competitive and dissatisfied. It creates inequalities and sets folks up to resent others.

We are working to eradicate this at our company. While we still do have some of these inequalities, we are fixing them as soon as we find them."

O "Success in the eyes of an engineer is cool technology. Success for finance staff is profitability. Success for manufacturing is that our products are easy and inexpensive to build. Success for procurement is that it's easy to buy the parts that manufacturing needs. All too often, each department has different criteria for success. And that's what employees get rewarded for. They aren't rewarded for how the organization does overall. That isn't a good thing."

O "One CEO I worked with believed in creating competing engineering groups. The winners make out well and others lost. It created a cutthroat culture. Sales groups stole sales from each other. Service groups did too. The CEO was brilliant in other respects, but this system didn't work at all. We didn't care what other companies were doing; we were going to kick the 'blank' out of our other departments."

THE TAKE AWAY

Not all of the companies have perfect incentive systems. They are all works-in-progress. Some of these organizations have greater awareness of the need to reward collaboration, and their programs are farther along than others. The common theme here is an awareness that most of the leaders had, that their incentive systems need to encourage the right behaviors. They are willing to keep moving their incentive systems increasingly in that direction.

APPLICATION

Think about what incentives are common for your industry and at your company. Do your incentive systems reinforce employees who work hard and achieve stellar results? Do your compensation, bonus, and other monetary and non-monetary rewards reinforce collaboration? If yes, are they effective in encouraging employees to work with others? Where do your company's incentives fall short?

(12)

ACCESS ENABLES COLLABORATION

Access enables collaboration. It's that important. For any type of collaboration to be successful employees need easy access to others. If this is not a defining feature of your culture, then working together will be thwarted. This chapter will focus on the final Company Practice: fostering an environment in which employees can access coworkers with whom they need to collaborate.

Three critical topics will be covered under the umbrella of "access." The first is using physical office design to enhance collaboration. Specialists in industrial office design are teaming up with organizational psychologists to help leaders design workspaces in fun ways that increase employee productivity and teamwork. According to Ben Waber, a PhD from MIT who has built a successful career in this area, "Physical space is the biggest lever to encourage collaboration. And the data are clear that the biggest driver of performance in complex industries like software is serendipitous interaction."[1]

The second topic is how employees transcend distances in order to collaborate with others. Geographic dispersal might mean working across the state, the country, or the world. It might mean being located in adjacent buildings on a corporate campus. In some companies just working on a different floor of the same building creates a barrier to effective collaboration. "Dispersal" is in the eyes of the employee.

Even if your company has limited geographic dispersal of employees, this chapter can still supply you with some great ideas for increasing the effectiveness of collaboration.

The third topic relates to working at home.

Let's start with a story about how one of my Silicon Valley interviewees took the initiative to get better ongoing access to colleagues at the health center where she worked in order to provide the best possible care to patients.

TAKING INITIATIVE TO ACCESS COLLEAGUES MORE EFFECTIVELY

Twenty years ago, when I began working as a surgeon at Kaiser Permanente, technology was much less advanced than it is today. Because of that, I didn't have immediate electronic access to reports, write-ups, lab results, and other information I needed to review before appointments with patients. I would seek out the patient's primary physician to talk about the diagnosis that led to the referral. I would similarly seek out the radiologist, oncologist, and any other specialists to get test results and insights from those doctors regarding their interpretations of the results.

There was a lot of running around, and one-on-one consultations with this colleague and that colleague. It was important to do and was standard practice at Kaiser, and, I presume, at most health care institutions. Though it wasn't hugely efficient in today's standards, it was necessary and effective for the time.

Not long after that, I and some other colleagues realized that it made more sense for us to meet regularly as a group to discuss patients referred to us for specialized care. Instead of having sequential conversations about a patient, we could all participate in one conversation together. It allowed us to share our findings, interpretations, and previous experience related to that health matter. Others could understand what our views were based on and ask questions that were illuminating. We felt it would benefit patient care and also give us a way to share knowledge and learn from others.

We began these group meetings and found them both professionally valuable and personally satisfying. We met over lunch because that time worked for many and were delighted when it aided us in unexpected ways. "Breaking bread" together helped us get to know each other better. It also made it easier for us to disagree or make requests that might be perceived as unnecessary if made in another venue.

We anticipated that six specialists would form the core group that met weekly. However, when word spread about this meeting others asked to join. Our weekly meeting grew to around 20 professionals, including primary care, surgeons, radiologists, other physicians, nurses, counselors, and others involved in the care of the patients we are discussing. When members are not available to join in-person, they often join using phone or Skype.

The group is diverse not only in professional titles and job duties, but also in ethnicity, nationality, age, and gender. Having these larger numbers of attendees from highly diverse backgrounds has helped the effectiveness of the group, and benefits both the patients and the attendees. Over time, we have come to understand other's roles, needs, and styles better.

Our agreements allow us to coordinate care and avoid sending patients back and forth between health care providers. It's much better for patients when we avoid this shuttling, and it reduces frustrations between us as well. Our guiding principle is that patient care is always our primary concern.

The fact that the group still meets regularly today is testament to its effectiveness. We would not still be meeting if it wasn't highly worthwhile, especially since technological advancements have supplanted some of the original reasons for this group's formation.

THE TAKE AWAY

This story from Kaiser is a great example of employees accessing others to improve their work and provide even better patient care. Most of them worked in a cluster of buildings in close proximity to each other. They needed a space that could accommodate 20 people and the equipment to connect colleagues who could not attend in person. They also needed a meeting format that helped them to be successful. The main thing they needed was a commitment from each of these extremely busy health care professionals to make this meeting a priority.

DESIGN YOUR PHYSICAL SPACES WITH EMPLOYEE INPUT

Although these medical professionals at Kaiser do not need to speak with each other daily, many people in other companies need frequent interaction. Physical space configurations can make a big difference when it comes to effective collaboration. Many leaders in Silicon Valley have realized this, and have concluded that the cost of redesigning workspaces is well worth the money when it brings employees together more effectively.

It is becoming increasingly common for companies to create different workspace designs to meet the needs and desires of various employee teams. One Silicon Valley leader summed this up nicely, saying: "Comfort helps collaboration. People fight over the thermostat. If engineering wants it at 65 degrees and legal wants it at 75, you have to figure out how to do that."

Some companies pay significant attention to physical space design to encourage employees to spend more time at the office and make it more comfortable for them to do it. Google, for instance, offers employees at their East Coast headquarters in Manhattan: "[g]ourmet cafeterias that serve free breakfast, lunch, and dinner; Broadway-theme conference rooms with velvet drapes; and conversation areas designed to look like vintage subway cars. . . . The library [boasts] a bookcase [that] swings open to reveal a secret room."[2] Their headquarters campus in Silicon Valley is just as amazing, reflecting Google's commitment to "create the happiest, most productive workplace in the world."[3]

The attention and money that companies put into making their physical space fun, unique, and comfortable varies widely from company to company. Every company needs to decide what's right for their particular circumstances. There *is* a theme, however, that underlies this notion of workplace design, and I believe that it's stronger in Silicon Valley than in many other geographic regions and industries. That theme is a desire to make the physical workplace so comfortable that employees will want to spend long hours there.

Consider what some Silicon Valley leaders I spoke with had to say about physical office design. As you read these remarks think about whether any of their ideas might enhance your environment.

- "Our spaces are designed for collaboration. The look varies from building to building and depends on your work. Most buildings have rooms for stand-up meetings. Some have nice project space. Our individual work spaces are generally open work areas, cubes without the partitions. Our newer buildings have nice joint spaces— 'living room' types of comfortable areas, and meeting rooms. The only weakness of these arrangements is that you cannot leave the white boards full of stuff because they're a shared commodity."
- "As soon as we add new conference rooms they become very popular. Every time we build a new space we think about the best things to include (needed technology, etc.). This is especially important since some participants cannot attend meetings in person."
- "Our physical layout is a significant contributor to our culture of collaboration and its success. We have lots of open cubicles between the different groups. It makes it convenient if someone from finance wants to meet with someone from marketing. It makes conversations easier and more effective because they have a place to sit and chat. While this open configuration has drawbacks

(other people can overhear things that you may want to remain private), overall it works great for us. There are pluses and minuses of any set-up. You have to decide what you want and then make it work."

○ "Our environment is not individual offices, its all cubes. One group recently decided they wanted a true open-space environment that wasn't even cubes. We did it for them. They also wanted an all-glass board that they could write on. It cost a bit of money but it's worth it if it improves productivity. If it works for them, we'll be open to doing it with other groups who may also want it. We won't impose it, though. If different groups want different physical spaces, that's fine."

○ "If a group wants one of our smaller meeting rooms for an extended period of time, they tell facilities and it becomes theirs for that time (for instance, if marketing wants a war room for a brand campaign). But staff cannot leave stuff in big conference rooms when they leave for the day. We also have private booths that seat from one to six people. Open space is available on every floor; comfy couches and chairs, monitors near windows, white boards, etc. We have lots of glass and white boards to write on. They can be used by anyone."

○ "The physical environment is super important. Giving staff their choice; making the space work for them. People are at work for a really long time and it has to be comfortable. I've seen some companies that have bikes and scooters to get between buildings or even between floors. We haven't tried that but might at some point."

○ "The state-of-the-art regarding office space seems to have gone from individual offices to open space (cube-land). It's like that here; wide open space with desks. Personally, I think the 'no office' concept is less effective. Different people have different work styles, though; some folks need more quiet and others need less. This open style does have advantages in many other ways. The bottom line is that it is hard to design something that meets everyone's needs."

○ "We try to get folks to sit cross-functionally. Get finance to sit with their clients. It's hard. They like sitting with other finance folks. They feel they need to interact with their peers even more frequently than their clients."

○ "It's easier for staff to work together in these shared spaces. Folks shout to others; they communicate more. It's different than it was 10 years ago."

○ "We probably need to do a better job with this. We are realizing how important spaces are, and are doing a better job of tailoring to each group's desires as we redo buildings. We are not leading-edge in this regard, but we are learning."

○ "We intentionally have conference rooms with glass to emphasize transparency so as you walk by you can see whatever is on the projector."

○ "Physical offices are almost always designed thoughtfully. But not from a central philosophy. Most of our spaces are quite open, except for some senior executives or HR staff who need privacy. They have the few closed offices. Generally, people sit out in the open with desks. We have some private spaces with desks and phones that you can go in and use."

○ "I don't think I've seen any closed private office spaces here. There are meeting rooms and temporary offices to work if you need privacy, but not private offices. Most of the floor plans are very open. We will create customized spaces that can be reserved for the length of a project, if that is what a team needs."

○ "Our buildings have a lot of open space and meeting areas. But there's no prescribed way of doing it. Every team gets a space. Generally, it's cubed space. Engineers tend to get desks. But you don't have to work at your desk. You can find any space that works for you. Sometimes you need quiet to concentrate. I encourage folks to go wherever they need to get their work done well."

THE TAKE AWAY

Ideally, workspaces should be designed to meet the needs of both individual employees and groups within your company. Some employees benefit from regular ongoing interaction. In those instances, companies have found that workspaces in an open configuration encourage spontaneous conversations that result in better products.

Other employee groups benefit from frequent interaction that isn't necessarily continuous. They don't need to sit within earshot of each other. One person may realize they need a quick brainstorming session with several colleagues, and contact them asking if they can meet somewhere convenient. The physical needs of a group like that often are met with comfortable seating in a relatively quiet area, equipped with a white board to capture their thinking.

Companies that employ more than several hundred employees in different disciplines (engineering, operations, market research, sales, finance, human resources, and so on) are likely to find that they need a variety of workspaces.

There are a number of ways that you can obtain information about the physical set-up that will best meet the needs of your groups of employees. Internet research will provide ample information on this topic. Or you can hire a professional in the growing field of workplace design.

One of the things I consistently found in speaking with Silicon Valley leaders is that they involve their employees in discussions about how they want their workspace to be designed. Soliciting input from your employees will provide you spaces that best meet their needs, and assure staff that their views are important.

APPLICATION

Does your company do a good job in regards to designing physical spaces? Are they designed to maximize both productivity and comfort? Are they designed to meet the needs and desires of specific groups? Do they bring together the right people? What can you learn from the experiences of these Silicon Valley leaders that you can apply in your company?

GEOGRAPHIC DISPERSAL WORKS BETTER FOR SOME THAN OTHERS

Whether to have employees in different geographic locations is a controversial topic from a number of viewpoints. It raises questions about the cost of maintaining workplaces in more than one location. If locations are in different countries it can raise a host of questions including: language, cultural, and time differences between employees who need to work together; physical and cyber security issues; and socio-political issues regarding the employment or contracting of workers from other countries. These challenges are often counterbalanced by the very real cost savings associated with moving some functions, for example the call center or some coding groups, to regions with lower costs of personnel. Also, when two companies merge, their bases are usually not next door to one another, and key employees are often rooted in the two distant communities.

Some believe that hiring staff in different countries increases greater productivity. Having personnel who work in a wide range of time zones can extend the hours that the company is able to be productive. This often allows projects to move faster by creating two or even three "shifts" of work among professional disciplines.

Having staff located in other countries can also make it easier to understand other cultures in terms of customizing products to meet the needs of their citizens. Having local sales staff can make it easier to sell products in those countries. There are many other good reasons to have staff in other countries or in different parts of the country beyond the headquarters location.

Others believe that the productivity gained from geographic distribution is offset by communication problems and lack of continuity since employees cannot talk with each other as easily.

Let's hear the disparate views of some Silicon Valley leaders on the subject of geographic dispersal of employees. Ask yourself which of these perspectives makes most sense for your company.

- ❍ "In this firm, a high value is placed on co-location. You need to sit next to the folks that you interact with regularly. Especially between marketing and engineering. It's also true within and between other functional groups. We tell folks, 'No, you cannot work out of Denver just because you want to.'"

- ❍ "We do allow dispersal of sales staff. It makes sense for them to be closer to the customers. But we want engineering staff here working together and with others."

- ❍ "I'm starting to form the opinion that when collaboration is critical, you need folks to be co-located. I don't like distant code development teams that need to be connected to the mother ship. It's okay when you can divide the work and give those at a distance a separate portion of the project. Otherwise the 'tax' is too high. It's too hard for coders in the United States to stay in close touch with India or London. We do it. We use FaceTime, Google Hangouts, and other tools. But those are individual solutions, not group solutions. It's extremely hard for groups to have high-quality conversations at a distance. Technology just isn't there yet."

- ❍ "We have lots of non-co-located employees. We use Skype a lot. And other technologies. All of these tools have pluses and minuses. I'm in a worldwide position and have teams everywhere. I don't hop on a plane every day. But still, I am communicating with most of those folks all the time. Collaboration needs to happen. And work-life balance also needs to be factored in. As a manager, an employee, a mom, a coach, I need work-life balance. For me, I get the best balance by starting at 5 a.m. Nobody is asking me to do that. It's my choice."

- ❍ "This is profound for the future of our field. If we are short staffed, someone anyplace in the world can augment our staff. Someone in Afghanistan can help. It increases efficiency. We can scale up or down. You just have to remember that the same rigid criteria should hold for everyone though. You have to train remote workers to your quality and content standards."

- ❍ "We probably do six to 12 meetings per week here, about 500 per year. Lot of conversations, lot of conference calls, meetings. Because we are relationship based and because we're geographically dispersed, we are continually meeting with others."

- ❍ "Yes, we do have geographic dispersal of employees. When you have employees in so many places, we learned that their productivity goes way up if they meet face-to-face every so often. Creativity is hard to do remotely. It's much easier if they have gotten to know others. We have also learned that tough conversations are better handled in person. Once we met in London, because the topic was heated. We wanted to look each other in the eye. It was important. It created a much higher level of trust. And we are convinced that the results were much better than what likely would have happened if the meeting had been by phone or video conference."

THE TAKE AWAY

Is geographic dispersal of employees worthwhile? It depends on a number of factors. Can the work can be isolated into separate segments? If not, can parts of segments be completed seamlessly by employees who are not in close proximity to each other? There isn't one easy answer to this question that holds across a diversity of products and companies.

You may want to seek information from others in your industry who have already gone this route. Connecting with a professional organization in your field can provide content from the experience of others. If your firm decides that geographic dispersion is desirable or necessary, the challenge will be to ensure that your organization's Collaboration Ethos bridges the distance.

 APPLICATION

Are there distances between employees who need to work together at your company? Do your leaders acknowledge those distances and do things to help employees overcome the disadvantages of working at different locations? Are your company's actions sufficient so that employees can work together well from a distance? What else might make it better?

TELECOMMUTING WORKS BEST IN COMBINATION WITH IN-PERSON TIME

The topic of geographic dispersal also includes work-at-home options. This concept has both supporters and detractors among the Silicon Valley leaders I spoke with. Those in favor of telecommuting believe that employees are more satisfied and more productive when given the option to work from home. They also feel that working at home can reduce distractions and interruptions. Others see it as a perk that increases employee commitment to the company, either when it is offered regularly or just occasionally, such as when an employee needs to be home for an air-conditioner repairperson.

The data isn't conclusive from the standpoint of the bottom line. Having a significant number of employees telecommute can mean a smaller office and lower rent. Yet, it also typically means increased technology costs to equip employees to work effectively from a home office. Detractors point to the burden of managing employees who are not in the same location, and the challenges employees may have in working with each other.

Once again, let's tap into the wisdom of our Silicon Valley leaders. You will see distinctly different views from different people. They may provide your company with some new perspectives on the topic of telecommuting.

- ❍ "There are no strict company rules on this. I'd feel very uncomfortable hiring someone who was mainly going to work at home, though. I'd allow it one day a week. But we need regular face-to-face contact to get things done. I expect people to come in when they need to."

- ❍ "We allow staff in some positions to work at home and it will probably increase."

- ❍ "We do allow working remotely; for employees much more than managers. Managers need to be in meetings most of the day and that's too hard to do remotely."

- ❍ "Yes, we allow both managers and individual employees to work remotely. Telecommuting does make collaborating and other factors of organizational life a bit more challenging. We have Skype and video conferencing in some offices. We have recruiters in several different states. I never see them. We have engineers in numerous places too, including internationally. They come in once in a while, not very often. It's working. It depends on the job and the location as to how well it works. It's just the way the world has gone."

- ❍ "To work remotely, you have to realize that there is both 'good' and 'evil' technology. Evil technologies are the ones people hide behind (you cannot see my face in email, so I may blast you and run). Or we may go through 20 interactions before we get to agreement.

Good technology includes video. You see my face and we can interact in a rich way. You also have to spend a little money and bring people together at times. That human interaction is important; it's a false savings to not allow it. You learn much more about others when you are face to face. Having a personal relationship increases trust and enhances collaboration."

❍ "Yes, we do allow it. At first it was very hard to get folks who were working or managing remotely to feel part of things. They felt isolated. We had to work hard to get them engaged. It has taken two years of effort. We've had to consciously create opportunities. It's starting to be more effective. One thing we've learned is that some face-to-face contact is critical. Either they come in to work with us, or we go to them. That's made all the difference. And it *is* an investment. Not just in the activities, but in getting people to buy into it. We've always had the needed technology. That's never been an impediment. It's these other (soft) issues."

THE TAKE AWAY

Telecommuting offers both employer and employee many benefits. You may find that it's a viable option for some or all of your employees. If it does have potential for your firm, you may want to encourage your leadership to pursue it.

If you do pursue it, I suggest you keep in mind that "[e]motional energy ebbs over time and must be renewed through face-to-face interactions."[4] There is also another important reason for bringing employees together occasionally. Experts validate that "[t]he brain is always scanning for risk . . . and among the things it uses to determine if someone is friend or foe are non-verbal cues."[5] Even the best technological tools do not provide the chance for people to carry out that assessment and to develop the bonds of trust that are at the foundation of collaboration.

SUGGESTED POLICIES AND PRACTICES

Here are a few of the important policies and practices that companies typically put in place if they decide to offer telecommuting options.

1. Create an overall telecommuting policy. Identify which positions allow it, and with what frequency. Identify what requirements need to be attached to which positions, such as the acceptable work hours, and how communication with other employees will be handled. It's also very important to identify which positions will be exempt from work-at-home.
2. Share these policies with employees as appropriate. Let employees know that these policies might need to change and that work-at-home privileges are not guaranteed indefinitely.
3. Create a process for employees to apply for telecommuting.
4. Determine how you will figure out whether telecommuting is effective for certain positions and for specific employees who try it.
5. Determine when you will bring employees together for face-to-face interaction.
6. Create health and safety policies related to work-at-home and ensure that employees' home spaces meet those criteria.
7. Check your company's insurance coverage for employees working at home and ensure that your policy is sufficient.
8. Figure out what equipment an employee working at home will need, and who will be responsible for procuring and maintaining it.
9. Ensure that employee technological devices meet your company's standards regarding security.

APPLICATION

Does your company allow employees to work at home? If yes, how well does it work? Does it affect the ability to work well with others? Based on what you have read in this chapter and your own experience, do you believe your organization would benefit from any changes in your current policy?

(13)

COLLABORATIVE ETHOS: THE SECRET SAUCE IN THE SVAC

Some of us have had the good fortune of being on a team that really jelled, where our individual intelligences combined to form a powerful communal brain. As a result, the team achieved so much more than anyone thought was possible. Now, imagine that experience describing an entire company rather than just a rare team here or there. Imagine if this could describe your company.

Collaborative Ethos is the term I coined to describe the cohesive culture that can lead to previously unreachable success. A number of organizations in the Silicon Valley have this ethos. Yes, it is a result of concentrating on each of the three levels: individual skills, team tools, and company practices. But it's much more than that. Collaboration becomes a gestalt or central value that everyone embraces. It becomes a way of life that people prefer. Employees want to join forces with colleagues in their company rather than compete.

Spend time at one of these Silicon Valley firms and you'll find that there's a palpable difference in the way employees act with one another. It's not just that they are willing to pause their work to lend a hand to others. It's not only that they leverage their collective intelligence. They also experience the synergy that results when a whole organization shares that cohesive philosophy. They understand that they are more likely to create, for example, an affordable and renewable energy source or a mobile device that enables people to communicate more effectively. This helps the organization to succeed. It also makes it more likely that individuals will achieve their personal career goals.

At the end of Chapter 4, we saw how one multinational company puts it all together. Now, after examining each of the components of the SVAC in detail, let's examine the National Basketball Association's team in the San Francisco Bay area: the Golden State Warriors (GSW).

THE GOLDEN STATE WARRIORS: COLLABORATIVE ETHOS IN ACTION

As winners of two NBA Championships in a three-year period, the Golden State Warriors have amassed a fan base that extends far beyond the SF Bay area. Why? It is partially because they win. It is also because of the way they win and the way they run their organization. Under the leadership of Majority Owner Joe Lacob, President Rick Welts, General Manager Bob Myers, and Head Coach Steve Kerr, and a team of men who demonstrate genuine caring for each other along with their amazing athletic prowess, this organization is exemplary in its approach. Together, they are forging a "transparent, laid-back, egalitarian environment that has fostered a fun, free-spirited, pass-happy brand of basketball."[1]

Thousands of articles have been written about the GSW, highlighting the way they bind their individual talents into a unified team that is tough to beat. What follows is a portrait of the Warriors and how they exemplify the Silicon Valley Approach to Collaboration.

This example is separate from my interviews with Silicon Valley leaders. It is a picture of my creation after following them closely over the last several seasons.

THE INDIVIDUAL SKILLS OF THE TEAMMATES

BEING TRUE TO THEMSELVES

Anyone who becomes a professional athlete in the United States has much to be proud of. These individuals have different motivations. Many are chasing the money. Some want acclaim. Others are inspired by the chance to have a place in history by breaking records. Still others are pleased to have the opportunity to give back to their communities and be a role model for youth. Most like forging a successful career doing what they are great at. Whatever the motivator, becoming a professional athlete is hugely appealing.

But getting there isn't easy. As hard as we may find it to get the position we want in our work, it's that much harder to get a position on a pro sports team. The ratio between aspiring athletes and pro positions available is enormous. Getting one of those team positions requires years of rigorous practice and training. Keeping one of those positions requires a devotion to physical health and continual advancement of skills. Every athlete on the team demonstrates on a daily basis that he or she is true to him- or herself and their goals.

Draymond Green is a stellar example of someone who has learned to control his emotions rather than being buffeted-about by them. He has been nicknamed the "mom" of the team because of the way he unabashedly shows his heart.[2] In addition, he pushes himself to play with peak determination. The combination of these two factors got him in trouble in the 2015–2016 season. After accumulating a certain number of technical fouls (fouls are generally characterized by unsportsmanlike conduct), a player receives a one-game suspension. That happened to Green in the crucial fifth game of the finals against the Cleveland Cavaliers. And that turned the momentum. GSW lost the championship to the Cavaliers in Game 7.

Green vowed to not lose control of his emotions again and he lived up to that promise in the 2016–2017 season. Sam Amick, a sports writer with *USA Today* reported, "The senseless fouls that led to his ill-timed suspension back then are nowhere to be found now."[3]

Green credits his suspension with teaching him a big lesson. It was a wake-up call that convinced him that he needed to change. He mastered his emotions, learning to become even truer to himself. Green revealed: "It taught me a lot, so I appreciate it. I'm not one of those guys who's like bitter that something bad happens to me. I use it, take the lesson from it, and move on."[4] (I shared tips for harnessing your emotions, in Chapter 6.)

BEING TRUE TO OTHERS

The astronomical salaries paid to athletes are driven by the statistics collected by team management. The most basic of these stats is scoring: how many baskets a player generates for his team. On most NBA teams, a player's "points scored" are more important than his number of assists (passes to fellow players that lead those others to score a basket).

This has begun to change, however. Some owners and coaches have realized that simply maximizing individual scoring can be counter-productive to the team goal of winning. No team represents this way of thinking more than the Warriors. In the 2016–2017 season they set the league record for the most assists.

The Warriors have stars that came to this team after being "the man" on other teams. These stars willingly gave up their starting role—and with it the playing minutes needed to generate big time stats—in order to help their team in any way that was needed.

Additionally, the GSW have a number of players who have made it to the exalted All Star Game. But instead of only focusing on their own scoring, they take pride in setting up younger players to get points. The members of this team seem less concerned with padding their own stats than taking care of their teammates, both to facilitate the group's success and for the joy of supporting each other.

The Golden State Warriors are True to Others in many ways. When stars like Stephen Curry and Kevin Durant take a much-needed breather on the bench, television cameras regularly catch them wildly cheering their teammates on rather than focusing inward to regain their energy and contemplate the moves they'll make when they return to the court.

BEING TRUE TO THE WORK

Through the unending grind of summer workouts, preseason practices, an 82-game regular season, and a post-season that might last through June, the Warriors never lose track of the team's goal and their commitment to it.

At the conclusion of the 2016–2017 regular season, the Warriors were acclaimed for completing the best three-year record in NBA history. You'd think this would be a cause for celebration. But the Warriors knew that their true goal was winning the NBA Championship, and nothing short of that. Several weeks later, when they beat their first three sets of opponents 4-0, 4-0, and 4-0 in consecutive playoff rounds, they set yet another record for the best playoff start ever. You might think they would be celebrating at this point. But the team knew that their work was not yet finished; not until they finally beat Cleveland in mid-June did they feel like the task they had set for themselves a year prior had been achieved.

You cannot be truer to your work than that.

BEING TRUE TO THE COMPANY

"Company spirit" is not a phrase that usually comes to mind when thinking about how the players on most NBA teams spend their non-working hours. The millionaire stars of the Warriors, however, are as "rah-rah" about their "company" as any CEO could hope for.

On the verge of the Championship for the 2015–2016 season, the Warriors finished one game short of winning it all. Many employees, especially highly compensated ones, would move on to summer vacations, content with their individual achievement and compensation. Instead, over the 4th of July holiday in 2016, five players rented a house in the Hamptons to host a weekend with one of the premiere players in the league, Kevin Durant. Kevin's contract had just ended with the Oklahoma City Thunder, which meant he was a free agent and eligible to join any team. And he was being wooed by many.

Over the weekend, the teammates and some of the team's senior managers pitched Kevin. They talked about how the Warriors were a great organization. They said they were willing to give up some spotlight, some stats, and some salary to have him join their team and help make them even more successful. Kevin did join the team and the rest, as they say, truly was history. He contributed much to this team in the 2016–2017 season and won the Most Valuable Player award for his performance in the championship round.

How many of us have seen collaboration at that level in our organizations?

TEAM TOOLS

Kevin Durant has revealed that it was the communal soul as well as the communal brain of the Golden State Warriors that sold him on the team in the summer of 2016. "I was really looking for that energy, and I felt it from the beginning," Durant said. "It was just so pure. It was a feeling I couldn't ignore. I wanted to be a part of it."[5] He wasn't referring to the way the team played at their best. He was talking about the way they have bonded, worked together, and achieved excellence.

COMPANY PRACTICES

One factor in creating a Collaborative Ethos is for the organization to provide financial incentives that drive collaboration over individual achievement. Take a look at how the Warriors motivated and rewarded Andre Iguodala. In the four years prior to his arrival at

Golden State, Andre averaged 14.3 points per game and 5.9 rebounds per game. On the basis of these stats, Golden State paid Andre a base salary of roughly $12 million per year. For the four years that Andre played with the Warriors, he averaged 7.9 points per game (a 45-percent drop) and 4.0 rebounds (a 33-percent drop).[6]

In many firms, an employee with that kind of marked decline in performance would not be rewarded. But in July 2017, Golden State awarded Andre a new three-year contract, raising his base salary 33 percent to $16 million a year.[7] Why was he given this raise? For the past several years, the Warriors had asked Andre to sacrifice his starting role and his on-court time to strengthen the players coming off the bench who substitute for the starters. They also asked him to conserve himself during the regular season, so in the vital play-off games he had the energy to guard the oppositions' best players, like LeBron James of the Cleveland Cavaliers and Kawhi Leonard of the San Antonio Spurs. The Warriors did not base his raise on his individual stats. They based it on how well he worked with others to help the team win.

Also a factor in creating a Collaborative Ethos are the organization's management practices. Head Coach Steve Kerr is revered by the athletes who call him "Coach," by the owners and managers of the franchise, by colleagues in the NBA, and by the fans. Kerr has suffered from debilitating back pain for the last two years. At one point during the 2017 playoffs his pain got so bad that he had to remove himself from his role for 11 crucial games.

General Manager Bob Myers expressed the sentiments of so many when he announced Kerr's return to Game 2 of the finals with seven very powerful words: "I'll bet on him all day long."[8] Kerr was greeted with a standing ovation from the crowd in attendance that night when he surprised and delighted everyone by resuming his post as head coach.[9]

Kerr not only stands up for team members when he feels they have received an unfair call on the court, he also stands up for people who receive unfair calls in life. He is one of the sports leaders who "has emerged as a leading voice on social issues during one of the most polarizing times in the country's history."[10] His team appreciates this. Durant recently said, "He knows exactly what he's talking about. He's so informed and intelligent when it comes to topics, social issues."[11]

Kerr is unafraid to broach the tough topics whether it is in a private conversation with his team or an on-the-record interview with the press. "Within the past year, Kerr has publicly addressed gun control, Colin Kaepernick's national anthem protest, medical marijuana, President Donald Trump's rhetoric, and most recently Trump's travel ban on seven Muslim-majority countries."[12]

THE TAKE AWAY

All of these factors come together to create a Collaborative Ethos that is unique to the personalities of the Warriors franchise while also being emblematic of the Silicon Valley Approach to Collaboration.

What makes the Golden State Warriors organization have such a Collaborative Ethos? It's the collaborative spirit that typifies their management's actions on a regular basis. It's the personal values of the players that lead them to support each other rather than just advancing themselves. It's their commitment to community and people in need. And so much more. It's the combination of all of these factors that create the GSW unique Collaborative Ethos.

Any organization can create their own Collaborative Ethos.

 APPLICATION

Does your company have a Collaborative Ethos? If yes, take a moment to describe it. If not, is there a kernel of an idea that you could build on to help your company create your unique and inspiring Collaborative Ethos?

RECIPE FOR THAT SECRET SAUCE

Whether we are talking about the Golden State Warriors, the "Superb Software Company" highlighted in Chapter 4, or any other organization that has created that Collaborative Ethos, it is worth figuring out how they create that secret sauce of their unique Ethos. You've heard what Silicon Valley leaders have said. Now we are going to look at a truth about human nature. Why do people behave in ways that either foster or inhibit collaboration?

US VS. THEM

One of the characteristics of most of us humans is that we prefer to live and work in groups. That's not all we do, however. Once we are in a group, we look at others and determine whether they are in our group, which makes them one of "us" or not, in which case they are one of "them."

Experts have been studying this phenomenon for a long time and have come to the conclusion that it is human nature to look for clues when we meet new people to help us determine if that person is part of our own group or circle.[13]

This process of classifying people happens almost unconsciously, and once it happens it is hugely influential in determining how we feel about and treat others. When we decide that someone is "one of us" we have an instant emotional bond with them. We favor them over others who we don't have that automatic trust with.

Sometimes the determination of "us" or "them" is based on whether we believe we have common values and goals. At other times it is based on more subtle factors. Do we share a religion? An alma mater? A profession? A city in which we both grew up? On occasion it is based on more hidden factors. Does this person look or act like me? Are we the same gender? The same race? Do we speak the same language?

It's interesting that when we lack knowledge about others we still make these determinations based on factors that are sometimes quite ridiculous. One study found that "simply allocating people into arbitrary social categories, such as which of two modern painters they preferred, was enough to elicit ingroup identity, bias, and a degree of favoritism."[14] If fairly minor classifications like these can bring out such loyalties, imagine what can result from strong emotional bonding and/or philosophical differences about how to approach the work. For example, employees can become quite committed to the particular way their group intends to design a product, and might convince themselves that they deserve a greater voice in decisions than others who are also involved and just as knowledgeable.

This might seem discouraging. It is if we have only one primary group that we identify with, and if everyone else becomes "them." The good news is that it doesn't have to be this way. As far back as the 1930s, anthropologist Margaret Mead found that "a parliament of selves"[15] actually lives within each of us. The notion that we each have multiple identities is corroborated by both experience and social science. U.S. Senator Lyndon Johnson, for instance, once described himself as "a free man, an American, a United States Senator, a Democrat, a liberal, a conservative, a Texan, a taxpayer, a rancher, and not as young as I used to be nor as old as I expect to be."[16]

Teams that see staff from other departments as part of their circle are much more likely to collaborate with them effectively. For instance, Sally Smith is an engineer. It is possible for Sally to simultaneously see herself as a member of the project team that's developing the company's fantastic new digital camera, a member of the project team revising the vacation policies, and an esteemed member of the staff of this company (as well as a wife, mother, and female in her mid-30s who is a native of the Midwest).

If staff develop too strong an identification with just their small group (say, their peers in engineering) it blinds them from seeing that they are on the "same team" with the folks in operations and finance who are working with them to develop that great new digital camera. However, when they see their engineering group as just one team and identification, and also identify just as strongly with the larger project team creating that digital camera, then they all become part of "us." And when the project team revising the vacation policies also has a strong team identity then Sally and other members feel just as bonded to that team as they do to the camera development team.

Becoming aware of our multiple identities invites us to connect with and work much more effectively with many more people.

THE TAKE AWAY

There is a clear role for management in ensuring that individuals and teams develop multiple positive identities rather than clinging to a narrower, exclusionary "us" and "them" view of life. It is relatively simple to help staff develop multiple identifications at work. We just have to look for opportunities to inspire staff to feel bonded to all the teams they are working with and to the entire organization, and to see those memberships as fluid and subject to change when the project completes.

 APPLICATION

Do your leaders realize how easily 'us' cultures are created? Does your company effectively help employees see themselves as members of many teams? Try an experiment. For the next week or two, note how often staff use impersonal pronouns such as 'we', 'us', 'our', 'them', or 'they' when speaking of people in other teams. Also notice whether staff use the word 'us' or 'them' when talking about members of their own team. If your company is like most you're going to find that folks talk about their own group as 'us' and other groups as 'them.' This activity can provide you and your company leaders clues as to further work that might need to be done in order to create an 'us' culture at your company.

The next chapter will help you take everything you've learned in this book along with your workbook learnings, and use them to make meaningful change in your company.

(14)

THE END IS THE BEGINNING

By now it should be clear that individuals, teams, and entire companies benefit when they are committed to collaboration. Bob Mudge, president of Verizon, summed it up: "Collaboration is no longer just a strategy: It is the key to long-term business success and competitiveness. Businesses that realize this sooner rather than later will be the ones who win."[1]

The results from many collaborative efforts can be quantified. Recently, California chipmaker Xilinx "reported a 25 percent increase in engineer productivity by using tools that encouraged peer-to-peer collaboration."[2] Countless other quantitative and qualitative examples could be provided; many have been throughout this book.

You have read stories about how collaboration has made an enormous difference to Silicon Valley companies, their employees, and their customers. I have provided examples of companies that have been extolled for their overall approach to collaboration and for creating a unique Collaboration Ethos that fit their company's culture.

Now it's your turn.

CREATING THE STORY THAT DEPICTS THE STATE OF COLLABORATION AT YOUR COMPANY

I invite you to take everything you've learned and all the notes you've made and turn it into a story that depicts the State of Collaboration at your firm. The purpose of this is to create a report that you can use to talk with others in your company about collaboration. Use whatever format you feel most comfortable with and that is most acceptable in your culture. You don't have to spend weeks laboring over it, with the goal of producing a document worthy of publication. That isn't the purpose of this activity. When you have completed this work, you will have integrated your perceptions into a statement that highlights areas in which you are doing well and areas in which there are weaknesses.

With that story in hand, talk to your manager about the areas in which your company excels in collaboration. Talk about the possibilities for improvement. Engage in a dialogue to see if she or he shares your perspectives and your enthusiasm for making things even better. If they do, then figure out your next steps in helping your organization foster an environment where employees come together even better.

The following bullet points summarize the thinking and activities that I have suggested you undertake as you read the book. I have summarized key questions from each activity. In case you want to return to the area of the book that discussed each activity, I also included the chapter number (in parentheses).

Use this outline to remind yourself of questions that led you to meaningful realizations about your company. Those responses are the ones that you will want to capture in your report. Bring them together and create a story of how people work together currently in your company.

- ◐ **Defining collaboration.** What was your initial definition of collaboration before you began reading the book? Did your definition change after you read the definitions shared by Silicon Valley leaders and the

working definition of collaboration used in this book?
(Chapter 1)

❍ **Your company's definition of collaboration.** I suggested that you ask five colleagues how collaboration
is defined at your company. What do their responses
reveal? Do your company's views encourage or impede
effective collaboration? (You may want to include a
few highlights of those five responses. Including other
people's perceptions beyond your own may strengthen
your report.) If you haven't conducted that research yet,
it isn't too late to do it now. (Chapter 1)

❍ **When, where, and how is collaboration achieved
at your firm?** Are employees who represent different
areas brought together to create, design, and deliver the
products you provide to customers? Are they able to
combine their knowledge to create the best ideas? Are
coworkers brought together to brainstorm problems?
Are there certain groups who work better together than
others? (Chapter 1)

❍ **How important is collaboration to your company?** Do
you believe folks at your firm think collaboration is as
important to your success as Silicon Valley leaders feel it
is to their companies? (Chapter 1)

— Did you collect data about whether others think collaboration is vital to your company's success? What
composite emerges when you consider the responses
of those five people? What are the implications of
what they said?

❍ **What types of collaboration are most common at
your company?** (Chapter 1)

— Is your company in a highly controlled industry, a moderately controlled one, or one with few
controls?

— The three main types of collaboration are: 1) a few
hand-selected individuals coming together for a

specific task; 2) teams with special synergy that enables them to achieve great things; and 3) everyone being encouraged to work with others when it is appropriate. Does your company use all three types? Are one or two of these types more prevalent than others?

— If you tend to use only one or two of these types, might this hurt your company's results? How so?

○ **The six characteristics of collaborators:** The six characteristics are: 1) A Drive to Succeed; 2) The Desire to Contribute to Something Meaningful; 3) Persistence; 4) Acceptance of Differences; 5) Desire for Genuine Communication; and 6) Connection to Company-Wide Goals. (Chapter 2)

— Do you see any of these six characteristics represented at your company?

— Does your company use any of these characteristics to recruit new employees? To promote employees? Does your company conduct trainings in any of these areas? Can you see the value in doing so?

○ **The five core beliefs of collaborators:** 1) Some projects need assistance from others; 2) Group successes are gratifying in a different way than individual work; 3) The chance to learn from others is a chief benefit of collaboration; 4) The chance to teach is a chief benefit of collaboration; 5) Networking = collaboration. (Chapter 2)

— Which of these five are represented at your company? Your assessment will give you clues about how ready individuals in your company are to collaborate effectively.

○ **Three Stories of Successful Collaboration:** I presented three stories of collaboration: 1) Changing How the Product Is Delivered to Customers; 2) Grassroots

Product Development; and 3) Evolving How Work Gets Done. (Chapter 3)

— Do any of these stories offer ideas for ways your company can do things better? For instance, do leaders share enough context with employees so they can understand and buy into strategies, directions, and decisions? Are employees given the opportunity to research and present new ideas? How are big changes made in internal processes?

○ **The Silicon Valley Approach to Collaboration:** In a nutshell, the SVAC is a philosophy and a set of practices that foster a culture in which employees join forces when they can create better results working together than on their own. (Chapter 4)

— What aspects of the SVAC can currently be found at your company? Which of those aspects work well? What could be done differently to help you achieve the SVAC even better? Did reading about how it came together at Superb Software give you any additional ideas for things you could be doing at your company?

○ **Individual Skills:** The four Individual Skills are: 1) Being True to Yourself; 2) Being True to Others; 3) Being True to the Work; and 4) Being True to the Company. (Chapters 5, 6, and 7)

— Do employees use the four Being Trues at your company? Do you see one or two of them typically being emphasized more than the others? Or do employees consider all four areas in relation to each other when they are devising solutions to work challenges?

— Are there ways your company could encourage considering all four of these perspectives even more?

◑ **Agile:** An all-purpose process to guide and manage group projects. (Chapter 8)

— Does your company have some sort of all-purpose project management methodology which groups can customize and use to guide their projects? How well does it work? Does the information about Agile provide ideas for strengthening your process? Might you want to explore adopting this one?

◑ **Vital Team Tools to Help Groups Work More Effectively:** Several team tools were shared. They are: 1) Strengthening trust and respect between employees; 2) Framing topics clearly and precisely; and 3) Scenario Planning. (Chapter 9)

— Does your company help employees get to know each other better to build bonds of trust? Could they do more? Could the SanDisk model work at your company?

— Do employees at your company frame topics appropriately? Might some of the skills and tips provided in this chapter help?

— Could Scenario Planning help structure discussions on topics that are uncertain because of unknowns about the future?

◑ **Management Practices:** People-management practices have a profound effect on the effectiveness of collaboration. The following aspects are covered in this chapter: 1) Strategic business decisions that may have unintended effects on collaboration; 2) Management philosophies; 3) Values; 4) Inspiring visions; 5) Management practices; 6) Corrective practices; 7) Shared goals; 8) Organizational structure; and 9) How senior leaders work together. (Chapter 10)

— Does your firm have any strategies or practices that make sense from certain perspectives, yet have a negative impact on successful collaboration? If so, are leaders aware of the negative effect of these practices on collaboration?

— Do any of the management philosophies, values, practices, people-management strategies and corrective practices examples from Silicon Valley strike you as ideas that might help your company help foster increased collaboration?

— Do groups working together in your organization often have shared goals?

— In what ways does your organizational structure make it easier for people to work together? In what ways does it make it more difficult?

— Do your senior leaders work well together and with others, modeling successful collaboration at the top?

◗ **Employee Incentives:** Financial incentives reward employees for certain behaviors. Those are the behaviors that staff focus on performing well. (Chapter 11)

— Do your incentive systems inspire employees to work hard and achieve stellar results?

— Do your compensation, bonus, and other monetary and non-monetary rewards reinforce collaboration?

— Where might your company's incentives fall short in the goal of creating a collaborative culture?

◗ **Access to Other Employees:** Employees need access to each other. Included in this are: 1) Design of physical work spaces; 2) Fostering collaboration across geographic distances; and 3) Telecommuting. (Chapter 12)

— Are physical spaces at your company designed to maximize both productivity and comfort? Do those spaces encourage the right people to work together? Do the experiences of the Silicon Valley companies offer any ideas for your company? Are groups given input in designing their areas?

— Are there geographic distances between employees who need to work together at your company? Do leaders acknowledge those distances and do things to help employees work together from different locations? What else might they do?

— Does your company allow employees to work at home? Are they still able to work with others when needed? Do you believe your organization would benefit from any changes in the current policy?

▶ **Collaborative Ethos:** This chapter shows how some of the best companies have a distinct Collaborative Ethos that reflects their culture. (Chapter 13)

— Does your company have a Collaborative Ethos? If yes, take a moment to describe it. If not, is there a kernel of an idea that you could build on to help your company create your own Collaborative Ethos?

— Do leaders at your company help employees see themselves as members of many teams? Did you try the experiments suggested regarding "us" and "them"? What were the results?

Take time to organize and synthesize your responses to these questions. Summarize the key themes you notice as you read through the content. Where does your company excel? Where does it fall short? Make sure that the document you have created is as neutral and accurate a reflection of your company as you can make it.

Now it is time to meet and share it with your manager. If the two of you agree to talk with other leaders about improving collaboration, I recommend that you take one further action before you have those conversations. You can strengthen your story by creating a small task force of employees who are also committed to collaboration. Ask each of them to read the book. Then combine all of your perspectives into one composite report for leadership. The report will be more convincing if it reflects the views of a number of staff from various groups and from different levels of your firm.

If you would like assistance in pulling together the story about collaboration at your organization, feel free to contact me at my consulting firm, Critical Change.

Additionally, you may want to use an employee survey to gather widespread feedback on the current state of your culture. I have provided the following survey for this purpose.

AN EMPLOYEE SURVEY TO ASSESS THE STATE OF COLLABORATION

This survey can be used by employees individually to help them solidify perceptions of collaboration at your company. It can be also used by everyone in a group to capture their assessment of the state of collaboration within their own group, or at your entire organization. If every employee completes it, it can create a comprehensive snapshot of your company's collaboration culture.

INSTRUCTIONS FOR EMPLOYEES COMPLETING THE SURVEY

Some of the questions in this survey ask you to rate an item based on your own individual perspectives. Other questions ask you to provide a rating based on how most employees feel or the company's views. We realize that it's impossible for you to be certain how others feel about something. We are only asking you to share your perceptions of their feelings or company views.

Please use the following 1–5 rating scale: 1 = Almost Never; 2 = Infrequently; 3 = Some of the Time; 4 = Most of the Time; 5 = Almost All the Time

On a separate answer sheet, note your ratings for each of these 64 questions by question number and by section.

INDIVIDUAL SKILLS

A. Being True to Yourself

1. I am aware of my values and live in synch with them at work.
2. My current position is helping me move toward my career goals.
3. I am able to express my views in ways that they are heard and considered.
4. I understand how my feelings drive my behavior.
5. I express how I feel at appropriate times and in appropriate ways.
6. I manage my emotions rather than being buffeted about by them.

B. Being True to Others

7. I have a lot in common with others at this company.
8. I seek to understand how others feel.
9. Helping others is encouraged here.
10. We view disagreements as opportunities to explore diverse ideas and do not take them personally.
11. People here go beyond their own turf to pitch in and help get things done.
12. Staff are committed to doing quality work here.

C. Being True to the Work

13. We view our project's problems as our problems.
14. Employees learn and use their knowledge to create better ways of doing things.
15. We regularly adopt ideas shared by others.
16. We understand our customers' needs.
17. We are flexible and willing to adapt to new conditions.
18. Information comes through the proper channels rather than through the grapevine.

19. There is great interaction between my group and others with whom we work.
20. Given our priorities, we know what decisions are important.
21. It is clear who is responsible for making which decisions.
22. We know who must work closely together to achieve the priorities.

D. Being True to the Company
23. I can see how my work helps achieve company goals.
24. What happens in this organization is important to me.
25. Staff take pride in telling others that they work for this company.
26. People are committed to this company's directions and strategies.
27. When employees have to choose between doing what is best for their work group or the whole organization, they do what is best for the organization.
28. Employees are fine when it comes to adapting to changing conditions.
29. Leaders show they trust us based on the confidential information they share with us.

E. Team Tools
30. People share information openly.
31. We make a point of seeking ideas from others.
32. We encourage each other to openly and honestly say what we think.
33. Differences of opinion are used to explore ideas and reach better decisions.
34. We listen carefully to what others have to say.
35. We have work processes and tools that enable us to be effective.
36. We have a good, all-purpose process we use to guide project work.
37. Responsibilities and assignments are clear to groups that work together.

Organizational Practices

F. Management Practices

38. Our leaders help us understand the key business challenges this company faces.
39. Management trusts employees and shares relevant information and ideas.
40. Employees participate in making many of the decisions regarding work in their area, or provide input to those making the decisions.
41. Management in this organization works together as a team.
42. Managers foster collaboration between employees.
43. Management and non-management staff partner with each other.
44. We receive appropriate feedback on our work regularly.
45. Managers here deal with poor performance appropriately.
46. Our group and groups we work with have common goals and measures of success.
47. We have confidence in the fairness of management.

G. Employee Incentives

48. I know how my manager measures how good a job I do.
49. Doing a great job is rewarded at this company.
50. Each employee's compensation depends, in part, on how well they work with others.
51. Each employee's compensation depends on the results of both their group and other groups.
52. In the last 90 days I have received recognition or praise for doing great work.
53. My pay reflects the effort I put into my work.
54. Promotions in this organization are fair.

H. Access to Other Employees

55. It is easy for me to find and work with others when I need to.
56. Our technological tools make it easy for me to work with others who are not at the same physical location.

57. Our physical surroundings are comfortable and encourage us to want to spend time here and do our best work.
58. This company's practices regarding telecommuting are appropriate.

I. Miscellaneous

59. Employees identify with other teams as well as their own primary work group.
60. It's not about who came up with the idea, it's about selecting the best ideas.
61. I am an important part of this company.
62. We have the right people doing the right jobs.
63. The work we do here is important.
64. We have a Collaborative Ethos at this company.

FINAL SCORING

Review your responses to each of these 64 questions. Note any individual items that you rated less than 4. These are the areas that, if improved, could help improve your company's collaborative culture.

Now compile your section responses:

- ❯ Add the total of your responses to Section A together, then divide that number by 6. Note your overall rating for this section on your answer sheet.
- ❯ Add the total of your responses to Section B together, then divide that number by 6. Note your overall rating for this section on your answer sheet.
- ❯ Add the total of your responses to Section C together, then divide that number by 10. Note your overall rating for this section on your answer sheet.
- ❯ Add the total of your responses to Section D together, then divide that number by 7. Note your overall rating for this section on your answer sheet.
- ❯ Add the total of your responses to Section E together, then divide that number by 8. Note your overall rating for this section on your answer sheet.

- Add the total of your responses to Section F together, then divide that number by 10. Note your overall rating for this section on your answer sheet.
- Add the total of your responses to Section G together, then divide that number by 7. Note your overall rating for this section on your answer sheet.
- Add the total of your responses to Section H together, then divide that number by 4. Note your overall rating for this section on your answer sheet.
- Add the total of your responses to Section I together, then divide that number by 6. Note your overall rating for this section on your answer sheet.

Note any of the sections in which your answers averaged less than 4.0. These would also be great places to start working on improving collaboration at your company. Working on an item that scores less than 4.0 may mean making changes in that content area. Or it may mean that leaders need to do a better job of explaining to employees why that area needs to be that way at this company at this time. (That's what setting context is about.)

If you would like additional assistance in analyzing your survey results, feel free to contact me at my consulting firm, Critical Change.

FINAL WORDS

This is the end of our journey together. I hope that it's just the beginning of your journey toward helping your organization become a magical place in which employees join forces to create amazing things.

You can make a difference. Have fun with it. You now have what you need to help your company make a different kind commitment to collaboration. Your company can be the next Google. Or the next Golden State Warriors. Whatever a championship is for your organization, I am rooting for you.

NOTES

INTRODUCTION

1. Silicon Valley Competitiveness and Innovation Project, 18.
2. Ibid., 15–17.
3. Avalos, "Silicon Valley Innovation Economy Tops the U.S., but Perils Loom."
4. Snibbe, "Here's How Big California's Economy Really Is."

CHAPTER 1

1. LinkedIn Corporation, "About Us."
2. Ward, "Innovation and Collaboration are the New Dynamic Duo."
3. Cross, Martin, and Weiss, "Mapping the value of employee collaboration," 29–30.
4. Raconteur Media Limited, "Working Better Together."
5. Schrage, "No More Teams!" 31.
6. Gawande, "Big Med."
7. Associated Press, "Apple unveils first new gadget in nearly 3 years."

CHAPTER 2

1. Sullivan, "6 Talent Management Lessons."
2. U. S. Bureau of the Census, "100 Largest Urban Places: 1850."
3. Boudin Bakery, "Our story."

4. Levi Strauss & Co., "Our story."
5. J.M. Smucker Company, "The Folgers story."
6. Wikipedia, "San Francisco."

CHAPTER 4

1. Cikara and Van Bavel, "The Neuroscience of Intergroup Relations."

CHAPTER 5

1. Joseph, "To thine own self be true."
2. Tracy, "The Power of Self-Confidence," 6–7.
3. Joseph, "To thine own self be true."
4. Tracy, "The Power of Self-Confidence," 35.
5. Traugott, "Achieving your goals."
6. Bradberry and Greaves, *The Emotional Intelligence Quick Book*, 121.
7. Cosmides and Tooby, "Evolutionary Psychology: A Primer."
8. Cherniss and Goleman, *The Emotionally Intelligent Workplace*, xv.
9. Parker and Hackett, "Hot Spots and Hot Moments," 24.
10. *I Done This Blog*, "Google's Unwritten Rule."
11. Isaacs, *dialog and the art of thinking together*, 17.
12. Ibid.
13. Erickson International, "Commitment transforms a promise."
14. Wagner, "Mark Zuckerberg shares Facebook's secrets."
15. Quoteinvestigator.com says the originator was a Danish politician, Karl Kristian Steincke, who wrote this in the fourth volume of his multi-volume autobiography in 1948. (See *http://quoteinvestigator .com/2013/10/20/no-predict/*)

CHAPTER 6

1. These steps incorporate ideas from Brian Tracy, "The Power of Self-Confidence," The Intentional Workplace, "Living your values," and tips I have used over the years in helping organizations, leaders, and employees clarify their values.
2. TSNE MissionWorks, "The first step in resolving conflict."
3. Bradberry and Greaves, *The Emotional Intelligence Quick Book*, 39.
4. Ury, "Getting Past No."

CHAPTER 7

1. Bennet, "Knowing: The Art of War," 3.
2. Ibid.
3. Ibid., 5.
4. Elbow, *Embracing Contraries*.
5. Schrage, "Shared Minds," 34.

CHAPTER 8

1. Kavis Technology Consulting, "Why do we hate process."
2. Digité, "Why we hate process."
3. Agile Alliance, "Manifesto for Agile software development."
4. Agile Alliance, "12 Principals."
5. Agile Alliance, "Agile glossary."
6. SAFe for Lean Enterprises, "Lean-Agile Leaders."
7. Yatzeck, "How to control scope creep in Agile."

CHAPTER 9

1. See *http://quoteinvestigator.com/2014/05/22/solve/*, accessed August 2, 2017, for a detailed discussion of the origin of this quote.
2. Leeds, *Smart Questions*, 24.
3. Ibid., 27.
4. Schwartz, *The Art of the Long View*.

CHAPTER 12

1. Stewart, "Looking for a lesson in Google's perks."
2. Ibid.
3. Ibid.
4. Parker and Hackett, "Hot Spots and Hot Moments," 24.
5. Strategy+Business, "Your people's brains need face time."

CHAPTER 13

1. Slater, "Championship caps Warriors' three-year run of dominance."
2. Slater, "Think rings."
3. Amick, "Warriors' Draymond Green."

4. Ibid.
5. Slater, "Championship caps Warriors' three-year run of dominance."
6. See Basketball Reference, "Andre Iguodala" for Andre's playing statistics and Young, "Andre Iguodala" for his 2014–2017 salary information.
7. Wells, "Andre Iguodala, Warriors."
8. Kawakami, "Game 2 win is Kerr-fect."
9. Ibid.
10. Honda, "Warriors coach Steve Kerr."
11. Ibid.
12. Ibid.
13. Cikara and Van Bavel, "The Neuroscience of Intergroup Relations," 246–252.
14. Smyth, "Identity-based conflicts," 153.
15. Pratt and Foreman, "Classifying managerial responses," 18.
16. McQuillen, Licht, and Licht, "Identity structure and life satisfaction," 65.

CHAPTER 14

1. Mudge, "Why collaboration is crucial."
2. Haden, "Is collaboration still a key?"

BIBLIOGRAPHY

Agile Alliance. "Agile glossary," *www.agilealliance.org/glossary*

Agile Alliance. "Manifesto for Agile software development," accessed July 6, 2017, *www.agilealliance.org/agile101/the-agile-manifesto/*

AgileAlliance. "12 Principals behind the Agile manifesto," accessed July 6, 2017, *www.agilealliance.org/agile101/12-principles-behind-the-agile-manifesto/*

Altman, Louise. "Living your values at work," *The Intentional Workplace*, November 18, 2010, *https://intentionalworkplace.com/2010/11/18/living-your-values-at-work/*

Amick, Sam. "Warriors' Draymond Green: Last year's Finals suspension 'woke me up'," *USA Today Sports*, June 4, 2017.

Associated Press. "Apple unveils first new gadget in nearly 3 years," *New York Post*, June 6, 2017, accessed July 6, 2017, *nypost.com/2017/06/06/apple-unveils-first-new-gadget-in-nearly-3-years/*

Avalos, George. "Silicon Valley Innovation Economy Tops the U.S., but Perils Loom," *San Jose Mercury News*, March 2, 2016, updated August 16, 2016, *www.mercurynews.com/2016/03/02/silicon-valley-innovation-economy-tops-the-u-s-but-perils-loom/*

Basketball Reference. "Andre Iguodala," last accessed August 2, 2017, *www.basketball-reference.com/players/i/iguodan01.html*

Bennet, Alex. "Knowing: The Art of War 2000," ResearchGate.net, last accessed August 2, 2017, *www.researchgate.net/profile/Alex_Bennet*

/publication/275522457_Knowing_The_Art_of_War_2000/links
/553e976d0cf294deef7174d0.pdf?inViewer=0&pdfJsDownload=0&
origin=publication_detail

Boudin Bakery. "Our story," accessed July 6, 2017, https://boudinbakery
.com/our-story/#more

Bradberry, Travis, and Jean Greaves. *The Emotional Intelligence Quick
Book*, New York: Fireside, 2005.

Cherniss, Cary, and Daniel Goleman, eds. *The Emotionally Intelligent
Workplace*. San Francisco: Jossey-Bass, 2001.

Cikara, Mina, and Jay J. Van Bavel. "The Neuroscience of Intergroup
Relations: An Integrative Review." *Perspectives on Psychological
Science*, 9 no. 3 (2014): 245–274.

Cosmides, Leda, and John Tooby. "Evolutionary Psychology: A
Primer." Center for Evolutionary Psychology, University of
California, Santa Barbara, accessed August 1, 2017, www.cep.ucsb
.edu/primer.html

Cross, Robert L., Roger D. Martin, and Leigh M. Weiss. "Mapping
the value of employee collaboration." *The McKinsey Quarterly*, 3
(2006): 29–30.

Digité. "Why we hate process," Agile ALM, September 10, 2012,
accessed July 6, 2007, www.digite.com/blog/why-we-hate-process/

Dillon, Charlotte. "Google's Unwritten Rule for Team Collaboration,"
I Done This Blog, April 5, 2016, http://blog.idonethis.com/google
-team-collaboration/

Elbow, Peter. *Embracing Contraries: Explorations in learning and teaching*. New York: Oxford University Press, 1986.

Erickson International. "Commitment Transforms a Promise into
Reality!" blog entry by Teresia LaRoque, 7/3/2012, https://erickson
.edu/blog/commitment-transforms-a-promise-into-reality

Gawande, Atul. "Big Med," *The New Yorker*, August 13, 2012, www
.newyorker.com/magazine/2012/08/13/big-med.

Greene, Bob. "The First Step in Resolving Conflict: 'Go to the
Balcony,'" *TSNE MissionWorks*, February 13, 2014, http://tsne.org
/blog/first-step-resolving-conflict-go-balcony

Haden, Jeff. "Is collaboration still a key to success?," *Inc.*, February 14, 2014, *www.inc.com/jeff-haden/is-collaboration-still-a-key-to-success.html*

Honda, Dan. "Warriors coach Steve Kerr believes in leadership and criticizes the president for lacking that quality," *East Bay Times*, February 19, 2017.

Isaacs, William. *Dialog and the art of thinking together: A pioneering approach to communicating in business and in life.* New York: Currency, 1999.

J.M. Smucker Company. "The Folgers story," accessed July 6, 2017, *www.folgerscoffee.com/our-story/history*

Joseph, Stephen. "To thine own self be true," *Psychology Today*, April 11, 2013, *www.psychologytoday.com/blog/what-doesnt-kill-us/201304/thine-own-self-be-true*

Kavis Technology Consulting. "Why do we hate process so much anyways?" accessed August 2, 2017, *www.kavistechnology.com/blog/why-do-we-hate-process-so-much-anyways/*

Kawakami, Tim. "Game 2 win is Kerr-fect," *East Bay Times*, June 5, 2017.

Leeds, Dorothy, *Smart Questions: A new strategy for successful managers.* New York: They Berkeley Publishing Group, 1988.

Levi Strauss & Co., "Our story," accessed July 6, 2017, *www.levistrauss.com/our-story/*

LinkedIn Corporation, "About Us," accessed May 31, 2017, *https://press.linkedin.com/about-linkedin*

McNulty, Eric J. "Your people's brains need face time," *Strategy+Business*, December 12, 2016, *www.strategy-business.com/blog/Your-Peoples-Brains-Need-Face-Time?gko=31bdc*

McQuillen, A.D., M.H. Licht, and B.G. Licht. "Identity structure and life satisfaction in later life." *Basic and Applied Social Psychology*, 23 no. 1 (2001): 65–72.

Mudge, Bob. "Why Collaboration Is Crucial To Success," *Fast Company*, January 2, 2014, *www.fastcompany.com/3024246/why-collaboration-is-crucial-to-success*

Parker, John N., and Edward J. Hackett. "Hot Spots and Hot Moments in Scientific Collaborations and Social Movements," *American Sociological Review,* 77 vol. 1 (2012): 21–44.

Pratt, M.G., and P.O. Foreman. "Classifying managerial responses to multiple organizational identities." *Academy of Management Review,* 25 vol. 1 (2000): 18–42.

Raconteur Media Limited. "Working Better Together: A Study of Collaboration and Innovation in the Workplace," accessed May 31, 2017, *www.raconteur.net/working-better-together.*

SAFe for Lean Enterprises. "Lean-Agile Leaders," accessed July 6, 2017, *www.scaledagileframework.com/lean-agile-leaders*

"San Francisco," Wikipedia, accessed July 6. 2017, https://en.wikipedia.org/wiki/San_Francisco.

Schrage, Michael. *No More Teams! Mastering the Dynamics of Creative Collaboration.* New York: Doubleday, 1995.

———. *Shared Minds: The New Technologies of Collaboration.* New York: Random House, 1990.

Schwartz, Peter. *The Art of the Long View: Planning for the future in an uncertain world.* New York: Crown Business, 1996.

Sicinski, Adam. "Breaking down the five step goal setting process," *IQ Matrix,* accessed July 6, 2017, *http://blog.iqmatrix.com/goal-setting-process*

Silicon Valley Competitiveness and Innovation Project (SVCIP). "Silicon Valley Competitiveness and Innovation Project—2017 Report," accessed May 31, 2017, *http://svcip.com/files/SVCIP_2017.pdf*

Slater, Anthony. "Championship caps Warriors' three-year run of dominance," *East Bay Times,* June 18, 2017.

———. "Think rings, Green advises Bell," *East Bay Times,* June 24, 2017.

Smyth, L.F. "Identity-based conflicts: A systematic approach." *Negotiation Journal,* 18 vol. 2 (2002): 147–161.

Snibbe, Kurt. "Here's How Big California's Economy Really Is," *Bay Area News Group,* February 10, 2017, *www.siliconvalley.com/2017/02/10/heres-how-big-californias-economy-really-is/*

Stewart, James B. "Looking for a lesson in Google's perks," *New York Times,* March 15, 2013, *www.nytimes.com/2013/03/16/business/at-google-a-place-to-work-and-play.html*

Sullivan, John. "6 Talent Management Lessons from the Silicon Valley," *Ere Media*, November 4, 2013, accessed, July 12, 2017, *www.ere media.com/ere/6-talent-management-lessons-from-the-silicon-valley/*

Tracy, Brian. *The Power of Self-Confidence: Become unstoppable, irresistible and unafraid in every area of your life.* Hoboken, N.J.: John Wiley & Sons, Inc., 2012.

Traugott, John. "Achieving your goals: An evidence-based approach," Michigan State University Extension, August 26, 2014, *http:// msue.anr.msu.edu/news/achieving_your_goals_an_evidence_based _approach*

U.S. Bureau of the Census. "Table 8. Population of 100 Largest Urban Places: 1850," *www.census.gov/population/www/documentation /twps0027/tab08.txt*

Ury, William. *Getting Past No: Negotiating in Difficult Situations.* New York: Penguin Random House, 1993.

Wagner, Kurt. "Mark Zuckerberg shares Facebook's secrets with all his employees, and almost none of it leaks," *Recode*, January 5, 2017, *www.recode.net/2017/1/5/13987714/mark-zuckerberg-facebook-qa -weekly*

Ward, John. "Innovation and Collaboration are the New Dynamic Duo," *Forbes*, January 4, 2017, *www.forbes.com/sites /sap/2017/01/04/innovation-and-collaboration-are-the-new-dynamic -duo/#7271cbf44c2d*

Wells, Adam. "Andre Iguodala, Warriors reportedly agree to 3-year, $48 million contract," *Bleacher Report*, July 1, 2017, *http://bleacher report.com/articles/2704611-andre-iguodala-warriors-reportedly -agree-to-3-year-48-million-contract*

Yatzeck, Elana. "How to control scope creep in Agile," *Thoughtworks*, August 14, 2012, accessed July 6, 2017, *www.thoughtworks.com /insights/blog/how-control-scope-creep-agile*

Young, Royce. "Andre Iguodala agrees to four-year deal with the Warriors," *CBSSports.com*, July 5, 2013, *www.cbssports.com/nba /news/andre-iguodala-agrees-to-four-year-deal-with-the-warriors/*

INDEX

ABOUT THE AUTHOR

Thea Singer Spitzer, founder of Critical Change LLC, has been a consultant, strategic advisor, and coach to top executives and leaders for nearly 30 years (including 16 years with Microsoft). She partners in identifying and solving a wide range of tough management and organizational challenges.

She has received accolades and awards for her work with a broad array of industries including software, telecommunications, financial services, manufacturing, health care, utilities, and retail. Singer Spitzer earned her PhD in organizational systems from Saybrook Graduate School and Research Center and her undergraduate degree from the University of Michigan.

She resides and works in the San Francisco Bay area. To learn more about her, please visit *www.critical-change.com*.